Matthew M. Vriends, PhD

The New Australian Parakeet Handbook

Everything About Purchase,
Housing, Care, Nutrition, Behavior,
Breeding, and Diseases

With a Special Chapter on Understanding
Australian Parakeets

Drawings by Michele Earle-Bridges and Tanya M. Vriends

BARRON'S

D0452199

Front cover: Western rosella
Inside front cover: Crimson rosella
Inside back cover: Red-winged parakeet
Back cover: Red-rumped parakeet, Twenty-eight parakeet, Eastern rosella, Swift parakeet, Hooded parakeet

All inquiries should be addressed to:
Barron's Educational Series, Inc.
250 Wireless Boulevard
Hauppauge, NY 11788

International Standard Book No. 0-8120-4739-7

Library of Congress Catalog Card No. 91-35100

Library of Congress Cataloging-in-Publication Data

Vriends, Matthew M., 1937–
    The new Australian parakeet handbook : everything about purchase, housing, care, nutrition, behavior, breeding, and diseases / Matthew M. Vriends ; drawings by Tanya M. Vriends and Michele Earle-Bridges with a special chapter on understanding Australian parakeets.
        p.   cm.
    Includes index.
    ISBN 0-8120-4739-7
    1. Australian parakeets—Handbooks, manuals, etc.
    I. Vriends, Tanya M.   II. Earle-Bridges, Michele.
    III. Title.
SF473.A88V75   1992
636.6'865—dc20   91-35100
                                                     CIP

PRINTED IN HONG KONG

2345 4900 987654321

About the author:
Matthew M. Vriends is a Dutch-born biologist/ornithologist who holds a collection of advanced degrees, including a PhD in zoology. Dr. Vriends has written more than 80 books in three languages on birds and other animals; his detailed works on parrotlike birds and finches are well known. Dr. Vriends has traveled extensively in South America, the United States, Africa, Australia, and Europe to observe and study birds in their natural environment and is widely regarded as an expert in tropical ornithology and aviculture. A source of particular pride are the many first-breeding results he has achieved in his large aviaries. Dr. Vriends is the author of Barron's *Lovebirds, Gouldian Finches, Pigeons, The New Bird Handbook,* and *The New Cockatiel Handbook.*

Photo Credits:
Andy Cohen: front cover; inside front cover; back cover (Princess of Wales parakeet). G. Ebben: pages 19 bottom left; 20 bottom left, right; 37 bottom left, right; 38; 73 bottom left, right; back cover (hooded parakeet). B. van de Kamer: pages 9–10 top; 19 top, bottom right; 20 bottom; 37 top; 55 top right, bottom; 56 top, bottom; 73 top; 74 top, bottom; 99–100 top, bottom; 109 top left, right; 110; 111 top, bottom; back cover (Eastern rosella, swift parakeet). Paul Kwast: pages 10 bottom left, right; 55 top left; 109 bottom. Matthew M. Vriends: page 128; inside back cover; back cover (red-winged parakeet, red-rumped parakeet).

Important note:
The subject of this book is how to take care of Australian parakeets in captivity. In dealing with these birds, always remember that newly purchased birds—even when they appear perfectly healthy—may well be carriers of salmonellae. That is why it is highly advisable to have sample droppings analyzed and to observe strict hygienic rules. Other infectious diseases that can endanger humans, such as ornithosis and tuberculosis, are rare in parakeets. Still, if you see a doctor because you or a member of your household has symptoms of a cold or of the flu, mention that you keep birds. No one who is allergic to feathers or feather dust should keep birds. If you have any doubts, consult your physician before you buy a bird.
    Many insects used as food by birds are pests that can infest stored food and create a serious nuisance in our households. If you decide to grow any of these insects, be extremely careful to prevent them from escaping from their containers.

Contents

Contents

Preface

In Europe and in the United States, the keeping and breeding of Australian parakeets is one of the most popular branches of avicultural science. Thanks to the increasing breeding successes in the seventies, many species are now available, even to those fanciers with a tight budget.

Since the sixties, no more birds have been exported from Australia, that is with the exception of illegally smuggled specimens, which we also cannot discount. Thus fanciers in Europe and the United States can obtain mostly specimens that have been bred in captivity. Although, from an ornithological point of view, it is good policy to introduce new or "wild blood" into the captive stock, one also can say that birds bred in aviaries over many generations have grown accustomed to living in limited space and thus are readier to further continue reproducing under such conditions.

Although it seems that Australian parakeets are quickly being joined in aviculture by South American and other parrot species, it is our experience that there are great numbers of fanciers, at least in the United States, who keep and breed these wonderfully colored birds. It seems that the hobby is progressing in leaps and bounds. This book relates many experiences, and notes that originated during my study trips in Australia during 1962–1965 and 1981–1983 should be a very useful guide to the fancier, to the practical keeping, caring for, and breeding of Australian parakeets.

Although, from a scientific point of view, the budgerigar (*Melopsittacus undulatus*) belongs to the broad-tailed parakeet group, I have not included it in this book because there are already many good books available about this "comical" bird. I specially recommend Barron's *Parakeets* and *The New Parakeet Handbook*. Both of these books also provide further useful information.

This book deals briefly however with the cockatiel (*Nymphicus hollandicus*), in spite of the fact that there are also several good books about this species available—these include Barron's *Cockatiels* and *The New Cockatiel Handbook*. As this popular bird is regarded by ornithologists as a link between the broad-tailed parakeets and the cockatoos, I have considered it a good idea to include it here.

It is now more than ten years since I have given attention to Australian parakeets in an American publication. During that time aviculture has developed into a dynamic hobby; one only needs to think of the numbers of new mutations that have arisen in the last few years; particularly in the genus *Neophema*. I spent several years in Australia working on biological/ornithological matters and made intensive special studies of broad-tailed parakeets, a group of interesting, colorful, and frequently pleasant-voiced, nondestructive birds. Since 1958 I also have kept various species of Australian parakeets in my own aviaries. Thus I have had the opportunity to closely study captive groups of every species described in this book—and I have had breeding successes with many of them.

Many avicultural societies have assisted me in developing good methods of husbandry for our Australian parakeets, both in the United States and abroad. And for this, I am extremely grateful. Cage and aviary birds deserve to be protected and to be exhibited (via bird shows) so that interest in them is maintained and enhanced!

For many years bird societies consciously have distributed much information through meetings, lectures, popular and technical journals, exhibitions, and so on. They constantly have reported on new developments, but unfortunately have had to report on the extinction of a number of domestic birds.

The present increasing trend towards the keeping of all kinds of domestic animals is a praiseworthy phenomenon that can be considered to be essential to human life, or even to its continuing existence. People are still affected by the environment; the sheer happiness to be experienced by direct contact with "raw nature" is one of the most pleasant experiences humans can give each other.

Preface

I wish to thank J. Peter Hill, DVM, and Arthur Freud, for taking time from their busy schedules to review the manuscript, and for the valuable contributions they have made to the text. My heartfelt thanks also go to my friend John Coborn of Queensland, Australia, for the work he has taken off my hands, and to my talented friend, the artist Michele Earle-Bridges. My wife, Lucia Vriends-Parent, I thank for her moral support and her editorial and ornithological expertise. Last but by no means least, I thank my daughter Tanya, an art student at the University of Cincinnati, for her accurate illustrations.

As always, I am eager to receive any comments or constructive criticism that may arrive from anyone's reading of the text.

Loveland, Ohio   Matthew M. Vriends
Summer 1991

Soyons fidèles à nos faiblesses.
    For Lucia, my wife
    and Kimberly, my grandchild.

Management and Care

Considerations Before Purchasing

It is understandable that the acquisition of Australian parakeets (and all other cage and aviary birds for that matter), is often a matter of trust. If you are like most buyers, you will visit various dealers first as you probably will not know the addresses of any breeders. However, by studying specialist avicultural periodicals or contacting officers of bird societies, even veterinarians, you may find some useful addresses. Wherever birds are obtained, it is important to inspect them from close quarters before purchasing. The premises in which the birds are kept also should be taken into consideration. If the cages and aviaries are overcrowded, dirty, and smelly, then take your patronage elsewhere. If birds are kept in clean, hygienic conditions, then your prospective purchases are more likely to be fit and healthy.

Your first impressions of a bird are important: see that it appears fit, that it has clean plumage, beak, and feet; that the eyes are bright and alert. Never buy birds that are molting. But this is not all; proceed with the greatest caution! Expensive birds that in the past have been found to be useless as breeding stock, and are in reality quite worthless, often fall into the hands of inexperienced fanciers. Such birds may look quite healthy and full of life, but get them in your aviaries and they will refuse to breed and indeed will fight with their own species, whatever the sex! You thus will have spent good money on worthless birds. It is clear, therefore, why the purchase of birds is a matter of trust and honor.

What then, can you do to avoid purchasing substandard or worthless material? It is not always possible for a dealer to guarantee a certain bird species, although most purchasers will want to know as much about its previous history and ancestry as possible. Thus it is always best to purchase young birds—then if one turns out to be bad we will at least know that we have taken a justifiable gamble. *Neophema* species, for example, breed at one year of age. If we buy older birds we can be sure that

nine out of ten of these are not good breeders otherwise they would not be for sale. This is often the case with birds originating from Germany, Belgium or England. Older birds are often no longer so colorful so are sold off cheaply.

Why shouldn't you purchase these older birds? The answer is simple: most old birds for sale consist of hens that are no longer fertile, sterile cocks, egg pecking cocks and hens, hens that do not feed their young once they have hatched, cocks that pester their hens to death, hens that lay eggs but refuse to incubate, and so on. Only buy young birds of which you personally know their method of breeding, rearing, and so on. Of course, there also may be difficulties in the purchase of young birds; how do we determine the sex for example? There are several methods now possible, although many species can be determined on the basis of external characteristics (see pages 83–139). Endoscopy, a medical procedure, is a scientifically accurate method of determining sex; this is carried out by a veterinarian. Experienced fanciers also can help by showing beginners the pelvic test. By feeling the pelvic opening with the thumb one usually can determine the sex; hens, especially those that have laid eggs, have a wider opening than hens that have yet to lay an egg. In general, one can say that birds with the

The correct way to hold a small parakeet (*Neophema* species, for example).

7

Management and Care

The correct way to hold a medium-sized parakeet (Rosella species, for example). (See also illustration on page 14: Trimming claws.)

pelvic opening almost closed are *usually* cocks. If you can gently push the thumb between the pelvic bones then you almost certainly have a hen.

As a principal tip, only buy birds from knowledgeable dealers or breeders and, if possible, take an expert with you. Sometimes one can purchase young birds that have not completed the molt and that are difficult to sex; such birds are under a year old. These can give problems; many birds under one year old do not have external sexual differences. Young cocks not yet molted often are similar to old hens and young cocks also are similar to young hens.

If at all possible make an arrangement with the dealer or breeder (preferably in writing) to exchange bird(s) that don't turn out to be the right sex. Never buy birds that are brothers and sisters.

Do not buy too many pairs; you don't want to be overpopulated. The best method is to keep each pair in a separate aviary; with a few exceptions, multiple pairs in an aviary will lead to quarrels, fights, and bad breeding results.

Take the following points into consideration when purchasing Australian parakeets:
• The birds must not have a lean breast.
• The breastbone must not stick out.
• The feathers around the vent must be dry.
• The plumage must give a sleek impression, as though it is treated with wax (some dubious dealers in the past really did this!).
• The droppings on the cage floor must not be thin and watery (no diarrhea).
• The eyes must be bright, alert, and unblemished.
• Each foot should have four perfect toes, no scaly feet and no broken nails.
• The bird must sit well balanced on its perch.

You should not be alarmed if say, one or two tail feathers are broken or damaged. Parakeets are natural climbers and they naturally will damage feathers in a cage or aviary. When placed in a roomy flight cage, these feathers will be replaced at the next molt. Never keep birds in too small accommodations, otherwise the males are likely to become infertile and useless for breeding. All birds described in this book require a flight cage of at least 10 feet (3 m) in length; in smaller aviaries you can expect poorer breeding results. In my experience the best breeding results can be expected when each pair has its own flight cage, a point that I raise once more to enforce its importance. It is possible to keep most Australian parakeets in outdoor aviaries (with, of course, a draft-free and rainproof night shelter) when temperatures fall below 59 to 68° F (15–20° C). However, I personally do not like to expose birds to freezing temperatures and keep them indoors in the winter in an unheated but frost-free bird room. However if you have an aviary that

The habitat of the quiet and unobtrusive turquoise ▶ grass parakeets is open forest and lightly wooded grassland, where they live in pairs or parties of up to 30 birds. They nest in hollow limbs or tree trunks. Typical ground feeders, turquoise parakeets eat primarily grass and other seeds.

can be kept reasonably warm all year-round, this is best.

Never put new acquisitions together in a community aviary in the breeding season. (Beginners to the fancy often do; they bite off more than they can chew.) *Each pair must have its own aviary or its own section of an aviary.* New birds should be placed in aviaries when the weather is mild and still—preferably early in the morning so that they have the whole day to grow accustomed to their surroundings and find the eating and drinking sites.

Some newcomers immediately get their beaks into the woodwork of the aviary and soft parts are destroyed in a short interval of time. However, metal strips placed over the exposed woodwork will reduce this damage to a minimum! (In general most Australian parakeets will leave the woodwork undisturbed.) A metal framed aviary will relieve you of this problem (see page 26).

When Should You Buy Birds?

The best time to purchase new stock is just after the end of the breeding season as soon as the young are independent. You can then choose the best specimens, and they will have time to accustom themselves to new surroundings before the beginning of the next season. This is especially important if a particular species is sexually mature at one year of age.

Another good point is that the birds are usually at their cheapest at this time. The outlay is thus smaller and the risky winter period is past.

Transport purchased birds in separate containers if possible—this will reduce accidents. Place

◄ Top: There are various mutations of turquoise grass parakeets of which yellow, olive, and pied are the most common. Bottom left: The elegant grass parakeet has benefited from land clearance and has extended its range, especially in Southwestern Australia. Bottom right: The splendid grass parakeet or scarlet-breasted parrot is very nomadic and operates in isolated pairs or small groups of approximately 10 birds.

Various bird carriers are available. Top right: A traveling crate must meet airline regulations for size. Cover the whole inside with indoor/outdoor carpeting for padding and warmth. A proper perch also must be included.

them in their new aviary in the morning if at all possible. Keep them for the first few days in the night shelter so that they learn where they should go at night; then the pop-hole to the flight can be opened.

Of course, birds can be acquired at any time of the year. But the best breeding results will be accomplished if you get them just after the breeding season. The nearer to the beginning of the breeding season, the less chance of successful breeding. Most Australian parakeets generally soon get used to our climate.

Newly acquired birds can be put with each other in their new accommodations without much risk. However, older birds can be aggressive towards younger ones. Never put a hen directly with an aggressive male; he could persecute her and ultimately kill her. Put them in separate flights or cages next to each other so that they can see and get used to each other. The hen should be placed first in an aviary, the cock a couple of days later.

Management and Care

Take into consideration that aggression is a natural phenomenon that occurs in the wild with competition for food, suitable partners, nesting sites, and territories; and it is essential for the success of the species. In your collection, bear in mind that competition for partners is the greatest cause of aggression.

Cages

In order to keep parakeets in prime condition, good housing is a priority (see page 18). This means an aviary in which the bird can move about comfortably and that the fancier can easily keep clean. Birds with good housing usually become tame more quickly; the plumage keeps in good condition and color, the birds live longer and, if paired up, will breed quickly.

No cage is large enough for hookbills. Even the well-known budgerigar requires plenty of space. But there are times when you must consider using cages for one reason or another (sick birds, birds to be acclimatized, birds going to exhibitions, birds in quarantine). Cages should be constructed preferably from galvanized steel wire; wooden cages could soon be destroyed by the birds. There are many kinds of wire cages on the market, but the best are the rectangular types. The measurements for larger parakeets should be not less than 72 inches by 23⅔ inches (200 x 60 cm), with a height of 34 inches (85 cm); while the smaller parakeets can make do with 60 inches by 23⅔ inches by 34 inches (150 x 60 x 85 cm). These cages have a removable floor, making them very easy to clean without removing the birds from the cage. Some cages may even have a double floor, the upper one being a grid. Personally I am not keen on such a cage, though the bird cannot walk in its own dropppings. A compromise can be made by covering half of the grid with a grass sod, which is renewed frequently. Birds in such cages must be given a dish of grit once per week for one hour. Wooden cages will not be discussed here

Some common potentially poisonous houseplants that should be kept far from the birds: Top: caladium (left) and dieffenbachia (right). Bottom: azalea (left) and hyacinth (right). At the first sign of any abnormal bird behavior, consult your avian veterinarian immediately. Keep in mind, however, that birds may be able to tolerate more plant toxins than humans, dogs, and cats.

even if you are a do-it-yourselfer; even if you cover edges with a metal strip, sooner or later the cage could be gnawed beyond recognition.

Perches in the Cage

Perches are manufactured from hardwood, beech for example, and must not be too thin: ⅞ inch (22 mm). They also should not be too smooth; rough them up with coarse sandpaper at each cleaning. Birds have to rest on the perch and they cannot do this if it is too smooth and too thin. The bird must be able to spread its toes and such that the feet do not grip right round the perch. The perch should be round in section and the top (if you can have a top on a round stick) should be somewhat flattened, to help control growth of the toenails. Use hardwood because parakeets often are good gnawers and would destroy soft perches in no time at all. Also, soft wood is an ideal breeding ground for parasites, bacteria, and similar. Too thin perches have the disadvantage that the toes hang down and are not protected by the belly feathers of the sitting bird; in frosty weather this could well mean the loss of toe tips, or even whole toes through frostbite. To give the parakeets something to gnaw at and to take their minds off the perches, give them a regular supply of twigs from willow, apple, pear, plum, or hazel. It is best to dry these out for a couple of weeks before giving them to the birds.

Bathing in the Cage

Not all parakeets are enthusiastic bathers, especially if kept in a cage. There are a number of commercial metal or plastic "bathhouses" on the market, designed to hang over the open cage door, but these are ignored by many species. They would much rather be placed outside and given a mist spray with a hose, or placed under a dripping faucet. This is easy with tame birds, but new birds should be tamed well before this is attempted or they may panic. In any case, ensure that the bird is dry before it retires for the night. In hot, sunny weather there will be no problems in spraying bird and cage (remove seed hopper), then allowing them to dry out in semishade before bringing them indoors again.

Seed and Water Dishes in the Cage

Seed and water dishes in cages are situated so that they cannot be fouled with droppings. They should be easy to service and should be cleaned daily with water and disinfectant. The seed dish must be dried thoroughly before refilling with fresh seed. In the aviary, one can use automatic feed hoppers, and shallow dishes for water. A cuttlefish bone in the cage is no luxury, it supplies the bird with important minerals, and helps keep the beak in good order.

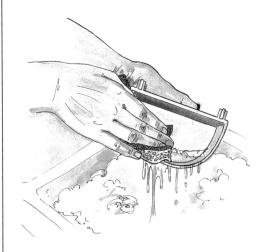

Keeping the birds' utensils—made from sturdy, nontoxic materials—scrupulously clean and disinfected (which means destroying infective agents like bacteria, viruses, and fungi) certainly will help decrease the possiblity of transmitting diseases.

The Right Spot for the Cage

The location of a cage with one or two parakeets is very important. Parrots and parakeets do not like to be left alone; they want to be in company and to hear things going on around them. The cage should be placed in a well-lit spot but not in the direct sun, there must be a possibility for the bird to get in the shade if it wishes. Beware! The sun moves around and there may be a point where the whole cage is in sunlight. Do not think that because a parakeet comes from Australia it likes to sunbathe for hours. A little sun and a little shade is the order of the day. Also, under no circumstances must the cage be put in a drafty position. Take care not to place it between two opposing windows or doors or in a hallway that opens directly outside. It is not necessary to cover the cage when night and day temperatures are similar.

Management and Care

Plenty of Space!

Australian parakeets are seldom kept in cages and are only really suited to aviaries; the roomier the better (the cockatiel is perhaps an exception). Australian parakeets are very accomplished flyers that will not remain healthy and fit in an accommodation that is too small. The following *minimum* dimensions are recommended for both outdoor and indoor aviaries:

• For *Neophema* species: length 10 feet (3 m); breadth 3 feet (1 m); height 6 feet (2 m).
• For *Platycercus* and similar species: length 13 feet (3.5) m; breadth 3 feet (1 m); height 6 feet (2 m).
• For *Alisterus* and *Aprosmictus* species: length 16 feet (5 m); breadth 3 feet (1 m); height 6 feet (2 m).

Perches in the Aviary

Artificial perches in the aviary also must be made from hardwood. Give the birds twigs to occupy them and take their minds off gnawing, so they shouldn't include each other's feathers! Fix the perches at each end of the flight cage so that the birds have a good flight path. Do not place perches too close to the mesh to protect the birds from cats, and to prevent birds from damaging their tails by continually rubbing against it. If possible, place an old tree trunk in the aviary or build the aviary around one, and see how happy the birds are with this arrangement!

Supply perches of various thicknesses to help exercise the birds' feet. There are perches that are fixed securely and those that sway. In the shelter it is best to have only fixed perches of suitable thickness for resting so that the birds are persuaded to go in at night. It is best to have these perches higher than any other perches in the aviary as the birds like to roost as high up as they can. Extra "climbing twigs," especially in the aviary corners, are useful, as it is usually a waste of time trying to grow anything in a parakeet aviary.

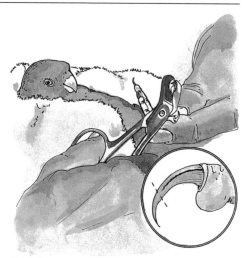

Trimming claws. Be careful not to cut the part that is supplied with blood ("quick"), but if the nail does start to bleed, a moistened stypic pencil, silver nitrate, iron subsulfate, or a liquid coagulant should be applied to the bleeding end. Note the proper restraining method, and compare this with the drawing on page 7.

Bathing in the Aviary

A large, shallow water dish should be provided in each aviary so that the birds can bathe if they wish. On cold days the bath should be removed. Take care that the birds are dry before they retire for the night; that means remove the bath by 4 or 5 P.M. If you have a lawn sprinkler, you can use that; many parakeets prefer a shower to a bath. A little pond with a fountain and running water is ideal, but expensive to install in each aviary. Never install perches above bath and drinking water. All water supplies must be replaced daily.

Drink and Seed Hoppers in the Aviary

The information given in the feeding chapter (see pages 27–39) applies as much to the fancier with a single pet parakeet in a cage as to the fancier who has several aviaries. However, birds kept in an aviary get more exercise and thus use more energy, so that oil rich seeds such as sunflower seeds, rapeseed, and peanuts can be given in relatively greater quantities. Seed containers must be virtually unbreakable, easy to clean and, if metallic, rust free. Wooden containers turn into splinters in no time at all and are totally useless. Several kinds of food containers or hoppers are available from the trade; ask your seed supplier for advice. Glass or ceramic hoppers are ideal and are the most used both for seed and for drinking water.

Locations for food and water hoppers must be chosen with care. It should be obvious, for example, that they are not placed in positions where they easily can become fouled with droppings. They also should not be placed in tight corners with room for only one bird to feed; this is bound to result in squabbling. The best place therefore probably is near the aviary center. The hoppers are best raised from the floor on platforms (a concrete slab raised

Heavy, nontoxic food and water containers are necessary for the larger parakeet species, and should be placed conveniently near the perches.

on four bricks is ideal). Cuttlefish bone, mineral blocks, and such can be fastened to the aviary wire within reach of the end of a perch, while grit can be supplied in a ceramic or similar container.

Catching Birds

If one needs to catch birds from aviaries for whatever purpose, never do this in hot weather when temperatures are above 77° F (25° C). High temperatures are likely to exacerbate the shock and stress derived from the capture, and can increase the risk of heart failure! *Neophema* species especially are susceptible to problems from shock in hot weather.

Birds should be captured with a good quality net of about 15¾ inches (40 cm) diameter; the framework of the net should be bound with foam rubber or something similar, to reduce risk of injury. Such nets are available ready-made in pet stores or from avicultural suppliers. I personally prefer a short-handled net made from cheesecloth or similar material. The depth of the net should be not less than 17¾ inches (45 cm) (see also page 16).

How Many Birds?

Most fanciers like to assemble a collection of several species and this usually poses no problem with the easy to obtain kinds. If possible it is best to obtain two pairs of each species you wish to keep. You can then make up unrelated pairs from the offspring. You also get a greater chance of successful breeding with two pairs and, of course, if one of the older birds should die prematurely, you can always replace it with one of the young from the other pair.

When purchasing young birds, always try to get two males and two females as unrelated as possible. All four can then be placed in an aviary. For identification you can mark the birds with a felt pen, or by clipping away parts of tail feathers. Frequently you will find sufficient differences among the birds themselves to help in distinguishing individuals; no two birds are exactly alike, there may be a difference in general body form, in size and shape of head, one nail may be missing, or a nail is bent, and so on.

As soon as you see that two birds are attracted to each other, then remove the other pair from the aviary. The more young birds you can acquire and accommodate in this manner, the greater the chance of forming good breeding pairs. Do not, however, keep more than a pair of birds together for longer than necessary, especially those species classed as aggressive.

If you wish to build up a good strain, you must follow the examples of budgerigar and canary breeders, who breed with several pairs, and select the best young for further breeding.

Are Australian Parakeets For You?

Captive animals, and that includes Australian parakeets, must totally rely on us for their welfare; they cannot fly off into the woods and look after themselves as they would in the wild. Indeed, escaped birds rarely survive for very long in alien climates and terrains. You must therefore be prepared to take the responsibility of looking after your charges. Every bird is an individual and the fancier must take the time to learn the requirements of every one.

For example, one newly acquired parakeet may be wilder than the next. This may have to do with the individual character of the bird, but it also can have a lot to do with the influence of the environment. A bird placed in a quiet spot, and spared the sight of battalions of humans, will be much shyer than a bird who sees a continual stream of people passing his cage. The best example of this is of birds in zoos and wildlife parks, in which there is virtually no question of shyness or fear, even with imported specimens. This also affects breeding; fearless (of humans) birds will breed and rear their young much more efficiently than shy ones. They will stay on

the nest more readily and will acclimatize to new surroundings very quickly.

It is no mistake therefore, at least outside the breeding season, to allow as many people as you can to inspect your birds. From my own experience I can say that children playing, after a time, make hardly any impression on the birds' behavior, as long as this, of course, is not allowed too close to the aviary! Tamer birds will not flee to the shelter so often and you therefore will be able to enjoy them more in the outside flight.

Go out of your way to get your birds accustomed to you; that will mean that they develop familiarity and recognition. Feed them at set times and they soon will get to know this and will welcome you. Always let them hear you are coming, especially when they are in the night shelter, as they cannot always see you. You can whistle a tune, sing, or talk, so that they get to recognize your voice and know you are on the way. Footsteps alone will not let them know who is coming.

Parakeets are able to recognize their keeper not only by ear but also by sight. My wife can thus hear from the birds that I have arrived home. Do everything as quietly and gently as possible and don't make sudden movements.

No fancier can escape the need of catching a bird from time to time. To keep on good terms with your birds, however, you should do this as little as possible. But there are occasions when you must catch them: treatment for parasites or diseases, moving to another aviary, selling or buying, removing youngsters, and so on. Try to make the moves as short as possible. Be sure of yourself, otherwise it can take a long time and the longer it takes, the greater the stress, not only to the bird(s) you are catching but to other birds in the aviary. Hide the catching net as long as possible because the birds may have seen it before and they don't forget that quickly!

As soon as you have the bird in the net, secure it so it cannot injure itself or bite you. I do not advocate the use of gloves as you lose the direct contact with the bird's body and you cannot feel how you are gripping it (see also page 14).

In their natural habitat, Australian parakeets would enjoy at least 12 hours of daylight per day. This is different in many other countries; in winter, for example, the birds could sit from 4 P.M. to 8 A.M., thus 16 long hours, in the dark. You must therefore supplement with artificial light. This is important because the birds already may have difficulties to acclimatize. Extra food is thus necessary to provide energy and enhance body heat. There are several kinds of lighting systems with time switches and dimmers on the market. See your avicultural supplier for details.

Housing

General Remarks

Many beginners, to their regret, build one or two aviaries without thought and planning for the future. It is much better to plan well in advance, to measure the available space and to use it with a view to expansion at a later date if necessary. Then, should you wish to increase the number of your aviaries, you can do so easily. When building aviaries you should bear the following three points in mind:
• The aviary must be suitable for the type(s) of birds you wish to keep.
• The aviary must be easy for the fancier to service.
• The aviary must complement your house and garden.

These points suggest that most Australian parakeets are kept in outside aviaries. They may be kept in indoor enclosures, but most fanciers do not have the room for large flights, and the number of species one can keep comfortably in cages is minimal. Moreover, there is no substitute for the benefit of natural sunlight and rain to the birds and their plumage.

In preparing the overall plan, there are a number of points you must consider. Firstly, the siting of the aviary is of prime importance; which compass direction should the front face? Many fanciers have little choice in the matter and are limited to the attributes of the available space; however, it is wise to bear the following in mind (these points pertain to the Northern Hemisphere):
• To the north: little sunlight, much cold wind and rain.
• To the east: mornings—good sunlight; in the afternoons and evenings—little or no sun; in the summer—dry winds; in the winter—raw, cold winds, no driving rain.
• To the south: much sunlight all day, driving winds and rains variable.
• To the west: no morning sun, afternoon and evening—adequate sun, much wind, driving rain, especially in the chilly and damp fall.

A combination flight and shelter suitable for various Australian parakeet species. Note the container drawer, which can be pushed inside the aviary when filled with treats or daily seed mixtures.

When planting and building, take these points into consideration. (The extent to which you can actually do so may depend on whether you live in the middle of a village or town, or out in the open country.) If the open part of your aviary faces south, you should consider planting some deciduous trees and shrubs to provide shade in the summer but to let through the winter sun. If you intend to keep red-eyed mutations, which are sensitive to strong sunlight, you certainly should consider planting to provide as much shade as possible from the stark summer sun. Never plant your trees or shrubs so close to the aviary that their twigs or branches can damage the mesh. Also, branches that hang over the aviary provide various enemies of the birds (cats, birds of prey, and so on) a better chance of approaching their "prey"; and, although they may not be able to catch them, they can spread alarm and stress among your birds. Regular pruning is therefore necessary to prevent mishaps. Take into consideration that a south facing aviary also has its

Top: Bourke's parakeets are from mulga country and ▶ sandy areas. They are excellent, unaggressive aviary breeders as long as only one pair is kept in the same enclosure. Bottom left: Swift parakeets breed only in Tasmania from November to January. After the breeding season, they cross Bass Strait to winter in Victoria. Bottom right: In the aviary red- or crimson-winged parakeets usually are very spiteful towards other birds.

An outdoor aviary consisting of eight single-pair pens: an excellent setup for breeding various Australian parakeet species. It is possible to enter each flight by a door at the rear of the first pen. There are low connecting doors between each flight.

disadvantages: hot summers will mean that the temperature in the night shelter can become too high. Provision of adequate ventilation is therefore a priority (but watch out for drafts!). Sliding panels, high in the walls and protected on the inside with wire mesh, are ideal.

As it is important to keep an aviary as draft- and damp-proof as possible, one with a north facing aspect is the least suitable. Many kinds of birds, for example splendid parakeets, are susceptible to extreme weather conditions. Damp aviary floors have the disadvantage of nurturing bacteria and worm eggs; *Neophema* species are susceptible to lung infections if kept in such conditions.

Personally, I find an east facing aviary to be good. The birds get early morning sun, and although this may disappear in the afternoon, the warmth will

◀ Top left: In Australia the uncommon Barraband parakeet is called superb parrot or green leek. A pair in an aviary is inoffensive and docile, and usually becomes extremely tame. Top right: Princess of Wales parakeets, from the arid interior of Australia, are easy to breed in captivity. Bottom: Lutino Princess of Wales.

stay for some time. The harsh westerly winds will pose no problems here, especially in the fall and winter. One disadvantage is the possibility of cold easterly winds in the winter; these are not so frequent and should they occur, I shut my birds up in their night shelters for protection.

A west facing aviary poses similar factors to the east facing aviary, but in reverse. One can protect the birds by covering a large part of the roof of the outdoor flight.

In addition to the climatic conditions, a number of other factors must be taken into consideration. A good view of the aviary from the house has advantages but the aviary must be protected from noise (as at a party, for example), light (automobile lights for example), and so on; although birds soon can become accustomed to regular disturbances.

All in all the prospective fancier must come to terms with his own situation, in which finances also can be of utmost importance. Before you commence building, it is highly recommended that you visit as many other fanciers as possible. See how they have built and do not hesitate to ask for information and advice on anything you are not sure about. And don't forget the all important question: "What would you change if you had the chance to rebuild your aviaries?" One doesn't learn just from positive experiences but also from negative ones!

The general picture you will get from most other fanciers is that the aviaries are built to a certain standard pattern: 3 feet (1 m) wide flights in adjacent rows, not necessarily with separate entrances to night shelter and flight. Most trees and shrubs are planted outside the aviaries as most parakeets will destroy those planted inside.

Do not accept the opinion that smaller parakeet species necessarily can make do with smaller aviaries. The *Neophema* species, for example, travel huge distances in the wild and thus do better in as large a flight as possible. Also, better breeder results are obtained in aviaries rather than cages. Additionally, *Neophema* species are very susceptible to fat-liver disease and gout if they receive too little

Housing

An outdoor aviary with two flights. Note the safety porch, which is an essential requirement to prevent the birds from escaping. All wooden surfaces should be covered with strips of metal, although the majority of Australian parakeets leave most woodwork alone.

exercise—a situation that can be avoided with a large flight.

Night Shelter

Before beginning to construct a night shelter, you must consider what functions this has to perform in your particular situation. The following tips will give you some ideas:
• sleeping quarters;
• protection;
• living quarters in adverse weather conditions;
• nursery;
• dining area.

Birds should be encouraged always to spend the night in the night shelter. Parakeets do not see well in the dark and they are scared easily. If they spend the night in the outside flight they are more likely to be panicked (by cats, owls, car lights) and fly full pelt into the aviary wire causing injuries of all categories; even a broken neck. It therefore is best to build the night shelter in such a way that it can be closed off from the flight. There are some birds that seem to prefer to go back outside even if you have driven them in for the night.

The door to the pophole to the night shelter should preferably have a remote control from out-side the aviary. A vertical sliding door mounted between two aluminium runners can be raised and lowered by a nylon rope affixed to the center of the top of the door and passing over runners (or preferably through a metal conduit to prevent gnawing) to the outside of the aviary. When the door is to remain open during the day, the rope is simply tied to a fastener; when the birds are inside at night, the door is lowered simply by releasing the rope. The door should be made of fairly heavy material so that it will fall easily and it should also be as gnaw-proof as possible. A similar, horizontal sliding door can be made to operate with a rigid rod passing to the outside of the aviary. The rod is hinge jointed so that it hangs at right angles down the side of the aviary when the pophole door is open. To close the door, the rod is brought up into a horizontal position and pushed.

Most birds like to roost as high up as possible. If the roof of the night shelter is higher than that of the flight, this will encourage birds to roost therein. If this is not the case, the birds should be locked in the night shelter for two to three weeks and they will then normally use it at night thereafter.

The night shelter protects against harsh weather conditions and during the day can give shade from the summer sun. Moreover, it provides a secure rest area.

Parakeets are naturally most active mornings and evenings as they like to fill their stomachs before and after the hours of darkness. During the day they generally rest quietly; in Australia, this is because the days can be exceedingly hot and it makes no sense to use a lot of energy in high temperatures. Many captive parakeets will sit most of the day in the shelter. Beware of drafts in the shelter; most parakeets are very sensitive to these.

During the colder winter days birds should be locked in the shelter. Although most Australian parakeets are frost hardy, it is always best to take precautions in the coldest weather. The mere closing of the night shelter door will ensure that the temperature inside is warmer than that of the outside; especially as the cold wind will have been eliminated. Although the night shelter need not be so big as the flight, it should be as large as possible to allow winter confined birds to fly around, an exercise that, in itself, will help them to maintain warmth.

The feasibility of artificial heating should not be overlooked. Most fanciers find heating is not necessary for their parakeets; but those who live in areas that fall to 20° F and lower should perhaps reconsider! Moreover, it is not pleasant for the attendant himself to feed and water his birds in such low temperatures. A little warmth also will ensure the drinking water doesn't freeze.

Not only will a little warmth make it more comfortable for birds and their owner, it will help fight an outbreak of disease and possible death. All fanciers with experience will know that statistics of sickness and death increase in the colder months from October to March. Such statistics can be moderated by giving the birds shelter from biting winds, fog, drizzle, and driving rains.

Methods of heating should be considered, bearing in mind that paraffin and oil are unhealthy, electricity is expensive, and gas has possibilities. Best, however, is to have the night shelter connected to the central heating!

If you are about to start building an aviary, it is best to plan for wiring, water pipes, central heating, drainage so that even if you do not require these services right away, they will be easy to install in the future if necessary.

The shelter is ideal for breeding birds; it is more peaceful and quieter than outside and night visitors will be excluded. The breeding process is easier to monitor and the temperature is more constant. If a nest box is outside it can become wet by driving rain or roasted by the hot sun, and temperatures can change suddenly.

The food also can be placed in the shelter to protect it from the weather. It is useful to have a running water supply leading into the shelter or service area, for cleaning and for drinking water.

Drinking water supplied in the shelter will not freeze in icy weather. An electricity supply will give lighting and power for hospital cages and other equipment.

With larger groups of aviaries, a passageway behind the shelters is almost essential. This can be very efficient and time saving when you are servicing your aviaries. You can make the service passage wide enough to hold a number of cages, whereas the nest boxes can be installed on the side nearest the flight. Entrance doors to night shelters should be as short as you can comfortably use, otherwise birds will tend to escape over your head (another good reason for having a service passage—if the outer door is closed, the escaped bird is still confined). A small sliding trap in each shelter will enable you to feed and water the birds without entering and disturbing them each time. The entrance door is used when you want to clean, tend nest boxes, catch birds, and so on.

In my own aviaries I like to have the floor of the night shelter raised about 3 feet (1 m) high. As each night shelter floor area is about 3 feet square (1 x 1 m) there is no need to use the whole vertical space. Indeed the birds tend to stay as high up as possible and hardly use the floor. Other advantages are that the floor is at a comfortable height for cleaning and the area below can be used for storing food, nest box equipment, and so on. Some fanciers even use the area below as emergency accommodations for birds.

The walls between the shelters and the service passage in my aviaries are made of mesh. Although the birds can see each other, this does not seem to lead to any problems. Aggressive species, however, should have a double mesh wall between the shelters (and flights). One advantage of mesh is that the birds can see you coming when you enter the service corridor; if the wall was solid, they would only hear you and not know what was coming—something to scare them unnecessarily. Another advantage is that one or two lamps in the passage are sufficient to light up the whole area; a single heater also will heat the whole area; impossible if the dividing walls are solid and, in both cases, there will be no need for electrical cables passing through the birds' accommodations. Of course, gnawing birds, like parakeets, must be kept away from all kinds of electrical installations or, sooner or later, a nasty accident will occur! If you heat the shelter, maintain the temperature only a few degrees above the outside temperature, otherwise the difference will be too great and the birds could start molting.

The Flight

The flight is attached to the night shelter and is constructed from wire mesh mounted on a framework. Aviary widths are similar and in most cases are 3 feet (1 m), especially as most meshes are available in this width. Frames should preferably be made 3 feet (1 m) wide to avoid much cutting during construction. The size of the mesh generally used is ½ inch (1.25 cm) square and 19 gauge. New mesh is usually quite dazzling, especially when the sun shines on it, so a coat of mat black or asphalt paint applied with a roller will help.

The framework frequently is made of timber, which is relatively cheap and easy to attach the mesh to. However, one disadvantage is that some parakeet species will gnaw the framework—sometimes even rendering it irreparable. If the mesh is attached on the inside of the framework, it will help to stop gnawing to some extent. However, it is much better to protect the inner woodwork with strips of metal.

Another possibility is to construct the whole framework with metal. This usually is more expensive and the mesh is more difficult to attach, but it will last much longer and the birds cannot destroy it.

If you have several adjacent flights, you have various possibilities of access. A service passage and safety porch along the front of the flights can be used. Or you can have a door leading from one flight into the next; but this often is not praticable as you cannot put a perch where the door is if the door

reaches the top of the cage and you will thus shorten the flight space. If the door is shorter you can have a perch above it, but it will be right in your path. The best way is to have the door in the center of the flight walls. Be sure to have reliable latches on the doors as parakeets are very "mechanically minded" and will visit the neighbors given the opportunity.

The drinking vessels can be placed near the front of the aviary; if placed on the floor they will be fouled quicker than if elevated. They can be filled easily with a hose or a watering can and, if a small door is placed in the mesh, they can be removed easily for cleaning without entering the flight. Do not place water vessels below perches.

Some fanciers cover their flights completely, others partly and yet others not at all. The first possibility will ensure that the birds will not get worms and it will afford good protection. One disadvantage is that in warm weather you will get a greenhouse effect.

Partly covered, the birds have a choice of sitting under shelter or enjoying the weather. It must be remembered that coverings of transparent plastic, glass, or plexiglass, will cut out the ultraviolet rays from the sun and will reduce the birds' ability to manufacture vitamin D. Partial covering of the roof will mean that nest boxes can be placed outside more safely.

Pests and Vermin

The aviary is constructed for your parakeets, but you will get other animals who will want to share the accommodations or get at your birds. Your main problems are likely to be mice and cats, but you may also have trouble with such animals as moles, rats, weasels, owls, and other birds of prey. In addition, we have the less obvious residents, such as bird lice and other insects.

Mice can be a major problem. They seem to get into every aviary at some stage or another. Young mice can easily get through your normal ½ inch (1.25 cm) square mesh and through the tiniest holes in your night shelter. Build an aviary with mice in mind. Make everything as mouseproof as possible and do not leave any dark corners for them to hide. Be sure that all cavity walls and insulated areas (the roof, for example) are completely sealed because once inside, the mice will be difficult to eradicate and can severely damage your insulation. Styrofoam, for example, is hopeless; mice seem to love to chew it up and, if you have a mouse infestation, you will find bits of styrofoam all through the aviaries.

Mice can be combated with various traps or poisons. However, mice can become immune to certain poisons if they are used continually, so the material should be changed from time to time. If the poison is left in open dishes, it should be placed outside the aviary. If used within the flight or night shelter, the poisons should be placed inside a bait box, with a tiny opening, large enough for the mice to enter but small enough to keep birds out. A heavy

Beware of mice and other uninvited guests! Make your aviary as mouse-proof as possible. Make sure that there are no dark corners or accessible cavities, which mice prefer.

brick placed on the box will render it more secure from disturbance by the birds. Be sure to keep an eye on this in case the mice drag the poison pellets out. Mice tend to use the same runs, and, if you can find these, a trap placed across the runs often will catch a mouse even without the use of bait.

Another possibility is to place dark boxes with just a small entrance hole. Because there is nowhere else to go, the mice may nest in these. It is then easy to shut them in and then to dispose of them. Sonic devices that emit high frequency sounds that rodents (as well as cats and dogs) can't tolerate provide a more humane alternative.

There is not much to say about cats. The best method is to install an electric shock wire. There are special apparatus designed for aviculture on the market. Agricultural electric fence apparatus or sonic devices also can be used and sometimes you may get these secondhand for a good price. The use of double mesh on the aviary will stop the cats getting at the birds but the shock element is still there. Cats can get used to the idea that they cannot get the parakeets and eventually will give up and take little or no further notice of them. In turn, birds can get used to seeing cats in the area regularly. However, if a strange cat suddenly should come near to the aviary, all hell may break loose.

Moles, rats, and weasels can gain entry if the foundations of the aviary are not deep enough, if the mesh is of too big a gauge, or if you have not taken enough care in vermin proofing. Though moles pose no threat, if weasels get in, you can say good-bye to your birds. Of course prevention is better than cure here and if a mishap occurs it is most likely because you have not taken the necessary precautions. Sonic devices have also been used effectively.

Birds of prey can sit on the roof of the aviary or dive at it. The greatest danger is that the parakeets will panic and injure themselves. Shock and related stress are also to be taken into consideration. Owls tend to avoid aviaries that have glossy, glazed white balls on the roof at night.

Bird lice and other parasites can be avoided by good hygiene and treatment with insecticides. Further information on the control of parasites will be found on page 63.

Aviary Construction

• If financially possible, I would recommend aviaries built of brick (foundation) with galvanized piping for framework. Add a solid concrete floor and you will have a durable and hygienic aviary. Use galvanized iron piping of $^{19}/_{32}$ to $^{25}/_{32}$ inch (15–20 mm) diameter, wire mesh ½ inch (1.25 cm) square, thin 19 G gauge, or one grade heavier 16 G for rosellas and similar birds that seem to derive pleasure from biting the wire! The night shelter can be made from brick, cement board, or timber.

Do not put a layer of gravel on the aviary floor. It will promote worm infestations that will be difficult to get rid of. Gravel will harbor feathers, food waste, seed husks, and droppings and form a breeding ground for other dangerous organisms. Most Australian parakeets forage for food on the ground.

Fanciers with a small budget can, of course, use cheaper materials as long as they are gnaw-proof. Waste timber can be used for the frame, and the walls of the night shelter can be made of plasticized board of $^{13}/_{32}$ inch (10 mm) thickness. The roof can be made of planks and covered with roofing felt.

• Some fanciers cover the top of the flight with fiber glass or PVC sheeting—both are excellent materials to protect against dampness and drafts.

• Ensure the foundation is rodent- (and other vermin) proof by extending it 18 inches (50 cm) below ground level. Alternatively, bury the aviary mesh well into the ground and bend it outwards to stop rats and mice burrowing in. If you add mesh (or even lengths of scrap iron or old bicycle frames) to a solid concrete floor during pouring, it will strengthen and help prevent cracking.

• All roofs or covers should extend over the aviary walls to prevent dampness and/or flooding.

• If aggressive birds are to be kept in adjacent flights, it is best to have double mesh between the flights; this will stop birds clambering on the wire, going for each other's toes, and so on.

• Do not use lead-based paints on any parts of the aviary. To be safe, only use paint that is classified as child safe. Never introduce birds to a cage or aviary until paint is thoroughly dry. Do not use whitewash as it contains harmful lime.

The Bird Room

This is really little more than an indoor aviary. It may consist of a room containing several separate flights, or the room itself is used as a whole aviary. Wire mesh can be placed over windows so that they can be opened for ventilation. A wire mesh safety porch is also a good idea.

Fanciers who breed color mutations are very much in favor of a bird room. Also it is ideal for tropical and subtropical birds. A few of the rarer species can be kept together with some smaller parakeet species (i.e., cockatiels) providing they are all compatible. Some of the larger tropical softbills and other expensive birds, such as Australian grass finches, do well in such a facility.

In many cases a bird room will be found to be more efficient and appropriate than an outside aviary, especially if you are lucky enough to have a spare room in your home that you can use for your hobby. Prior consideration is required with a bird room as much as that required for an outdoor aviary so try and get everything right at the outset.

The best kind of floor is one that is tiled (slate tiles of the type used on laundry floors are relatively inexpensive and ideal for this purpose). A thin layer of sand sprinkled over the floor will make it easy to sweep up droppings and to change it at regular intervals. Any plants in the bird room will of course, have to be kept in troughs or tubs. If you keep a spare set of plants, you can redistribute them at regular intervals so that they get regular periods of rest and recuperation.

Feeding and Food

Introduction

Only a small percentage of cage and aviary birds are fed according to their physiological needs, and many others are more or less forced to take items of food that they are not accustomed to. Take, for example, the various lori species that frequently are just kept alive with different seeds, when the natural diet of most consists mainly of nectar and pollen, plus fruits, blossoms, berries, buds, and—especially the smaller and medium-sized species *(Lorius, Trichoglossus)*—some insects and seeds. Indeed, lories and lorikeets play an important role in the natural pollination of many flowering trees and plants. In this respect, I like Rosemary Low's remark: "I feel strongly that anyone who is not prepared to go to the bother of providing lories with fresh nectar daily, should keep seed-eaters—or preferably not keep birds at all." The amateur bird keeper with just one or two birds is often the culprit who, usually through ignorance, will provide mediocre commercial packet seed and—sometimes—a few supplementary table scraps.

One of the most common faults is giving birds in *small* cages food that is *too* rich in energy. The natural result is birds that are too fat. This is especially evident in pet budgies (parakeets). Budgerigars weighing more than 1 ounce (30 g) can be regarded as obese and require a change in diet and much more room to move about! Unfortunately there are lots of budgies that weigh 1.8 to 2.1 ounces (50–60 g)! Dr. Shelden L. Gerstenfeld, VMD is accurate when he says such birds "would need a long runway to get off the ground." (I am convinced that there is a double meaning to this statement!)

Another error often made is giving a *monotonous* diet. This soon leads to problems—especially with the so-called seedeating species. This problem usually arises with single, tame, pet parrots or parakeets that are allowed to "eat at the table" receiving all manner of smoked, salted, or spiced items that really are totally alien to the bird and can do a lot of damage.

The proverb: "So many men, so many minds" is very appropriate to our fancy, especially with regard to feeding! One frequently may hear the statement that if a certain foodstuff "works" (meaning that the birds appear, for the time being, healthy), then one is on the right track! Is that really right? Would a gradual change in the menu (and I would emphasize "gradual") perhaps work even better, and encourage the birds to breed?

I can say with conviction that a good diet is one that keeps a bird at an optimal standard of health, full of energy and joie de vive. A good diet will guarantee a long, trouble-free life for all of your birds. As we keep the birds in our homes and gardens we must take the full responsibility of their care and management—including the provision of the best diet imaginable. If we are not prepared to do this, then we should not be involved with the bird fancy, at least never keep them in cages or aviaries!

Over the years, many bird foods from the native lands of the birds have been imported. These often are good, but some fanciers ignore the experiences of successful breeders and provide their own brand of food mixtures.

Nothing new is stated when we say that enormous research has gone into the nutritive requirements of agriculturally important animals. The poultry industry is of special interest to the bird fancier and many aspects of breeding, housing, lighting, behavior, and feeding can be related to our hobby.

In the wild, most species of birds occur in the various vegetated zones. This can be the edge of the forest, near to water, or where there is a great variety of trees. The forest itself is home to relatively few bird species, both in tropical and temperate climes. The most favored places are where trees, shrubs, expanses of water, and flat lands are all represented. Here the greatest variety of foodstuffs—seeds, fruits, and insects—will be found. Here there is less competition for food and each species will seek food in its own manner. Seedeaters will forage mainly

27

close to the ground, whereas insect eaters will dine in the tree foliage. A fish eater will have no competition from a nectar feeder, and all birds will live in peace and harmony—at least until the meat eater turns up!

Taking a closer look at the birds, we will observe that the different species are each adapted to their own methods of feeding and the foods they eat. This is apparent in the general build of the body, the shape of the beak, the tongue, the feet, and the wings. There also are (less obvious) differences in the digestive systems and the internal organs. We recognize the strong, practical beak of the seed-eater; the sharp, hook-like beak of the flesh eater, the narrow and somewhat curved beak of the insect and fruit eaters, and the broad, filtering beak of the water birds that remove small animals from the water. If we examine the feet of the various birds, we will find just as great a variety, designed to match the species' way of life.

The birds' wings are designed not only to enable them to fly, but also to help protect them against predators. Some species have wings designed for long periods of gliding or hovering; others have evolved means of flying backwards as well as forwards. Some birds have wings designed for swimming under water in pursuit of prey.

A well-developed crop is necessary for the breaking down of seed. In some birds, crop milk is produced for rearing the young. Birds that feed on soft or semiliquid food do not have a well-developed crop. Seedeating birds have a well-developed gizzard and stomach. There are some birds that do not possess a gallbladder.

What Is Food?

Food is a mixture of the materials that each organism requires for normal growth, reproduction, development, and protection against disease. Growth is the increasing in size of the body and comes about by cell division. The greatest amount of growth occurs in young birds as they develop, and as the plumage forms.

Food consists of a number of chemical components grouped under proteins, carbohydrates, fats, vitamins, minerals, and water—all of which are required in varying amounts—by every member of the animal kingdom. However, body constituents of various animals are closely related. For example, taking a chicken, a horse, a sheep, a steer, and a pig, we will find that the amount of moisture in the bodies is 54 to 60 percent; protein, 15 to 21 percent; fat, 17 to 26 percent, and ash, 3.2 to 4.6 percent. As an animal ages, the moisture percentage decreases and the fat percentage increases. Among individuals of a particular species, we will see variations depending on the kind of habitat in which it lives and the type, quality, and quantity of food it eats.

Birds require a diet containing energy, proteins, fats, minerals, vitamins, and water. A deficiency of one or more of these constituents will result in bodily malfunction. This can happen after a week or longer. In growing birds, these malfunctions usually will manifest themselves much faster than in adults. Each certain deficiency malfunction will, in most cases, show a particular symptom.

It is not always easy to estimate amounts of dietary constituents required by particular birds. In practice, deficiencies are often a combination of shortages of various items and it may be difficult to ascertain which items these are. Another complication of dietary deficiencies is that the weakened bird will lose its resistance to transmittable diseases and can become secondarily infected. Food items that a bird cannot live without are known as dietary essentials—items of food necessary to keep the body in good condition and allow it to perform its biological functions. Such items *must* be included in the diet that we give our birds, bearing in mind that captive birds have little choice in the matter.

It is not hard to determine which items of food are essential, but rather more difficult to determine *how much* of these items are required. Factors such as the type of bird, its activity, climate, time of year,

Feeding and Food

and so on will effect it. Breeding and egg laying, molting, and so on will see an increase in requirements. Some dietary constituents can be stored in the body and kept in reserve. Others must be consumed on a daily basis. If not, then after a short time, or eventually, a deficiency problem is sure to arise.

Food Requirements of Wild Birds

The availability of food in nature depends on the type of habitat in which a bird lives. The amount of available food will vary depending on the season and the climate so that, throughout the year, varying amounts of seeds, fruits, insects, and so on, will be available. It is a difficult and time-consuming task to study wild birds with regard to what and how much they eat. This can be done by examining the contents of the crop and stomach, but it does not necessarily give us a true picture, other than telling us what the bird has just eaten. We would have to examine the crop and stomach contents of many birds at all times of the year before we had a good general knowledge of the diet. However, as this would mean the death of large numbers of birds, it is a rather drastic and unacceptable method. The most acceptable method is careful study of the bird itself. General body shape, type of beak, and build of the alimentary canal will give us some good indications as to what it mainly eats.

We know that many so-called seedeating birds sometimes will take insects as well as seeds and fruits, depending on the requirements of the birds and the availability of invertebrates. As specialist feeders cannot change their diet so easily, some species take the drastic step of migrating to a different habitat that sometimes may be thousands of miles away from the original one.

Factors that Influence the Food Requirements of Birds

The food requirements of a bird are determined by its physiological condition, its degree of activity, and the demands of the habitat. The most important phenomenon is the requirement for energy that is supplied by the diet. Energy is essential for a bird to be active and to maintain its body temperature at an acceptable level when environmental temperatures are low. Should the body temperature of the bird become too high—or too low—its resistance will be reduced and it will be susceptible to all diseases.

Hunger and satisfaction are totally different aspects of feeding requirements. Indeed, some "foods" can satisfy the hunger, but the bird could starve to death within 24 hours.

The physiological demands on birds and their resulting dietary requirements are influenced by growth, breeding and rearing young, molting, and so on.

An adult, nonbreeding bird kept in a cage or a large aviary will, in each of these situations, have different food requirements. Much activity and a lower temperature will require more energy that must originate from the diet. The number of hours of sunlight also will influence the bird's behavior. The availability of insects to seedeating birds will bring a special enrichment to the diet. Molting birds lose relatively more body heat and thus require more energy. In addition, they will require larger amounts of proteins to replace feathers.

Birds in breeding condition will require more fats in the diet as reserve energy supplies. During incubation, when they leave the nest infrequently, these fats will ensure that the bird's body temperature remains constant. In order to manufacture the eggs, female birds require extra nutrients. An egg consists of 11 percent shell, 31 percent fat, and 38 percent albumin (proteinous egg white), plus small but important amounts of vitamins and minerals. At first, these substances are drawn from the current food and the body reserves, but in times of shortage, they are drawn from the body tissues themselves.

It is most important that birds receive a satisfactory quota of vitamins and minerals; a deficiency of one or more of these will lead to so-called deficiency diseases of one sort or another. This can lead

29

to sterility in adult birds, inadequate fertilization, dead nestlings, and loss of resistance to infectious diseases. The calcium required for eggshell manufacture can seriously weaken the bones of the mother bird if she receives an inadequate supply in the diet both before and during the breeding season. The eggshell consists of approximately 85 percent calcium carbonate. The quality of the eggshell is mainly determined genetically, but also is influenced by the number of eggs produced and the availability of vitamin D_3.

Newly hatched young may be *precocial* (leaving the nest almost immediately) or *altricial* (staying in the nest for some time while being cared for by the parents). Precocial birds usually are well covered with down feathers at birth, but hatchling altricial birds usually are naked and take several days to develop down feathers. The quality of food received by hatchlings is very important for optimum growth and bone and feather development.

At this stage it may be prudent to briefly discuss the manner in which parent birds feed their young. The papillae inside the beak of, for example the many finch nestlings, play an important part. In most cases, the parents swallow the seed first and allow it to soften in the crop, before it is regurgitated for the young. Some parrotlike birds deposit the regurgitated food so that the young can take it in the beak. Hummingbirds force a mixture of insects and honey directly into the gullet of their young. Pigeons and doves produce crop "milk," which the young take directly from the gullets of their parents.

At fledging time, young birds usually are not fully grown. Their further optimum development depends on a good balanced food supply, and this will have a permanent influence on the bird's feeding behavior later in life.

Birds can be encouraged to eat when they see other birds eat. The hunger signals in the mouth, throat, stomach, and crop show great mutual differences. The sense perception and the satiation phenomenon are both dependent on what takes place in the awareness or subconscious levels of the bird.

Factors that Influence Food Choices

Ground birds, such as poultry, quail, and ostriches possess relatively larger amounts of flesh than flying birds. The increased amount of muscle also requires a somewhat stronger skeleton to support it. A well-developed pair of legs and feet is required to support this mass. Flying birds are relatively much lighter than ground birds. Ground birds have a greater requirement for proteins, whereas flying birds require more energy producing foods.

Habit plays an important role in food selection and if one completely changes a bird's diet, this should be done very gradually. If, for example, a parrot will eat only sunflower seeds, it will be necessary to change its diet before it suffers from a deficiency disease. It is not stubbornness on the part of the parrot; it is more the fault of its owner who may have been too lazy to start the bird off with a greater variety of food. The change to a better seed mixture will take time and must be done with care. In Japanese bird breeding establishments, where birds are hand reared, the food usually consists of a mixture of boiled rice, soya meal, fish meal, vitamins, and minerals. Next, they receive a few extra things to make variety, and finally, they are weaned off gradually to a seed mixture.

Birds also recognize items of food by their appearance. If some birds receive pelleted food in place of a seed mixture, the size of the pellets will play a part in its recognition as a food item. Domestic fowl, for example, initially will refuse pellets that are larger or smaller than their usual rations, even it made of exactly the same ingredients. If the usual size is mixed with other sizes, the chicken will peck up the usual ones first! In this case, the memory of the "normal" pellet size plays an important role.

Changing over to rearing food or food concentrates requires care and patience. It is foolish to expect a parent bird to change suddenly to rearing food just a few days before its brood hatches.

Feeding and Food

The shape and size of the drinking vessel will influence the finding and drinking of water. The environmental temperature will influence the amount of water a bird drinks.

The character or species of bird often is related to its readiness to change its diet. Hobbyists frequently have great difficulty in getting parrots to change their seed mixture. If a change should become necessary, it must be done with much patience, care, and understanding.

A bird should like the food that is offered to it. Because we cannot give it the type of food it would get in the wild, we have to use a satisfactory substitute. Meat eating birds are first given pure meat, which gradually is mixed with the necessary vitamins, minerals, and other essentials.

Certain seeds are preferred to others. This may be due to the hardness (or softness) of the seed husk, or its taste. The amount of sugar in the seed can influence its acceptability.

The shape of the beak and the pattern of the digestive system also will, of course, play a role in the choice of food.

Feeding Captive Parrots and Parakeets

As we have discussed already, we do not know enough about the natural (wild) diet of many parrot species. It is impossible or at least very difficult to allow captive birds to forage for their own food, especially with the demands of the breeding season, molt, and so on.

Research has shown that many parrotlike species feed, in the wild, mainly on seeds and fruits. Some species, for examples lories and lorikeets, or the Kea of New Zealand, are special exceptions. The Kea, for example, uses its "pick-axe" beak to dig up roots, bulbs, and burrowing insects. Many large cockatoos and members of the genus *Platycercus* (rosellas, and so on) eat many insects, water snails, and worms in their native Australia

and in captivity usually will eagerly accept small pieces of red meat.

Psittacines have a characteristic method of feeding. Seeds are dehusked and the husk discarded, and fruits are peeled or skinned. Thus, the digestive system is not troubled with large amounts of indigestible fiber. Because parrots dehusk their seeds, it is best not to use automatic feeding hoppers as the fresh seed will become covered with husks and the birds may have difficulty in finding their food. Another well-known feeding habit of many parrots is the holding of larger food items in one of the feet and manipulating it as though "feeding from the hand."

The majority of parrots are natural seedeaters. Captive psittacines often have to make do with the several kinds of commercially available, dried, packaged seeds. This is, naturally, far from optimal feeding; in the wild the birds have the opportunity to seek out all kinds of fruits, leaves, buds, flowers, seeds, grasses, roots, bulbs, bark, and insects. Thus

Various seeds and pellets are used for feeding Australian parakeets. Top, from left to right: broad-striped sunflower seed, small dark sunflower seed, and rape seed; middle: safflower seed, oats, buckwheat, and hemp; bottom: canary grass seed, pellets, and white millet.

Feeding and Food

captive birds cannot live from seeds alone; they require a lot more!

Smaller parakeets feed mainly on grass seeds (oats, millets, wheat, canary grass seed, and so on); larger species also take bigger, oily seeds (sunflower seeds, safflower seeds, and so on). These oily seeds are very "fattening" and deficient in various vitamins, especially vitamin A. Unfortunately, birds also soon can become addicted to these seeds (especially sunflower) and, all too frequently, a birds may make one of them its staple diet, refusing all other food.

To make further variety in feeding, give your birds unripe seed, preferably still in the ear (ears of wheat, millet sprays, and so on) as they would find it in the wild. This is not always available, so another possibility is germinated seed.

Most parrots are partial to green food and fruit, but especially the Neotropical species, like the Amazons, that will gnaw greedily on fresh branches of willow, fruit trees, and so on. Many species will devour the buds, fresh twigs, and flowers of trees and plants. Many aviculturists give their birds the

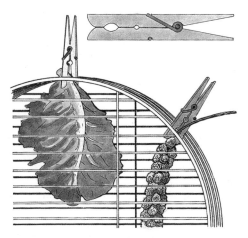

Wooden clothespins are helpful for clamping "treats," such as greens and millet sprays, to the trellis or mesh of cage or aviary.

seeds of leguminous plants (peas, beans, and so on), either fresh, cooked, frozen (thawed), or canned. Indeed, wild Amazons, for example, will rob legume plantations, much to the disgust of the farmers!

All psittacines require extra protein-containing foods during the breeding season. Excellent sources include meat (lean red meat, cooked poultry, pieces of fish without bone), cooked egg (yolk and white chopped in tiny pieces), small pieces of not too fatty cheese, cottage cheese, and yogurt. Raw or pasteurized milk is not recommended; although many birds will take it eagerly—for example stale bread soaked in boiled and cooled milk—some cannot stomach it too well and others may be sensitive to the milk's sugar content (lactose).

Unfortunately, birds newly out of quarantine frequently have been kept on a monotonous diet. It is the task of the new owner to introduce these birds to a more varied diet; in fact the more varied the better! Newly imported birds often are deficient in vitamin A. This vitamin is fundamental to the correct function of body cell metabolism, the maintenance of skin and mucous membranes, and the enhancement of sight. It also has an influence on the respiratory system, and plays a part in the pigmentation of the retina, thus allowing the eye to function well in poor light. Vitamin A is not only called the anti-infection or growth vitamin, it is also called the anti-sterility or fertility vitamin.

An Adequate Feeding Regime
For medium-sized parrots:
• oil-rich seeds, such as medium-sized sunflower, safflower, and a little hemp—especially during the winter and in the breeding season, or when birds are kept in unheated accommodations;
• leguminous plants, fresh and germinated;
• corn (softened and crushed), oats, wheat, various millets (especially millet spray, which is loved by all psittacines), canary grass seed, greens, fruits, fresh twigs, egg food, cottage cheese, yogurt, and so on.

Feeding and Food

For small parrots and parakeets:
• various small seeds (millet varieties—approximately 70 percent); crushed oats and canary grass seed to 25 percent and about 5 percent mixture of niger, hemp, poppy, and linseed;
• boiled egg, other animal protein sources, fruit, and greens.

All three groups can be given daily "snacks," such as diverse cereals (corn, wheat, bran, rice, shredded wheat, puffed wheat, rice, and millet), pieces of granola bar, and uncooked dry pasta. The latter can be given as a mixture in various shapes and colors; being curious, the birds are bound to try it and soon will eat it greedily.

The above is intended to enhance variety in the daily menu; one that is much safer than a monotonous one. That latter will be stressful and boring to the birds and will result in screaming and feather plucking, and they will seldom or never breed satisfactorily. A balanced diet in captivity means that the variety and quantity of constituents are such that they maintain the parrot in the best physical and mental health.

Food, a Summary

All animals, including Australian parakeets, require a balanced diet containing the constituent proteins, carbohydrates, fats, vitamins, minerals, and water.

Protein forms 50 percent of the dry weight of the body of any animal; in plants this usually is much less. Proteins are involved in all animal activity. In our birds they are important in growth, repair, and maintenance of all tissues including the feathers. In the breeding season, as the young parakeets grow, protein is of greater importance than in the winter, which is a rest period. Before they take on their new plumage for the winter after the molt, extra protein is essential, as protein is the basis of feathers. Proteins are built up from a great number of little building blocks, the so-named amino acids.

Some of these can be made by the bird itself, others must be present in the food. The food value of proteins is related directly to the essential amino acid content; that is, those that the bird cannot make itself. Most plant foods are poor in proteins, so the necessary animal proteins also must be made available.

Carbohydrates are necessary for producing energy and are an important part of the diet. In general, they originate in plants. They have no function with regard to growth or repair of cells, but are important for movement and maintaining body temperature. Grains and seeds contain a lot of carbohydrate, usually in the form of starch; sugars are also carbohydrates.

Fats and oils also provide energy and protection, and can be stored as a reserve of food. In the winter, a layer of fat is good for our birds. It will help keep them warm and can be used as food in an emergency.

Vitamins in small amounts are important for the maintenance and normal functioning of the body and its organs. They give no energy but are essential to life itself. Parakeets require various vitamins to enable them to reproduce and grow and to stay healthy. Vitamins are taken as part of the diet and are used in the breakdown and manufacture of proteins. In nature, vitamins occur in various forms; today they also are manufactured artificially.

Minerals are inorganic or nonliving materials that the bird needs for growth and maintenance of the body. The most important minerals are salts containing calcium, phosphorus, sodium, manganese, copper, potassium, iron, and iodine. Each of these has its own function(s). The term trace elements often is used to describe those minerals that the birds need less of.

Little need be said about the importance of water. The bird's body consists of more than one half water. Not all parakeets drink a lot of water. Birds from drier environments can go longer without water as they get their moisture requirements from the food they eat.

Feeding and Food

Cuttlebone can be purchased in your pet store. If you gather it on the beach, soak it for 24 hours; change the water every 8 hours. Cuttlebone contains about 81.5 percent calcium carbonate, and all birds will take it readily.

In addition to the dietary constituents mentioned previously, grit and gravel are important. Grit and cuttlefish bone can help supply the bird's calcium requirements to build bone, eggshells, and so on. This is then very important in the breeding season. Small grade gravel has the function of grinding up the food in the stomach, making it easier to digest. The gravel is not digested, but it passes through the body once it has worn too smooth to continue its job.

A Standard Menu

By looking around and seeing what is available commercially and what can be found in the wild, it will not be difficult for the average fancier to put together a suitable menu for his birds. As the parakeet fancy has boomed in recent years, commerce has found it lucrative to produce all sorts of appro-

priate products. The following is a summary of what psittacine birds should be fed in order to give them a balanced diet and ensure that they remain in the best of health through all natural phenomena:
• a seed mixture. There are various commercial mixtures made especially for larger parakeets and these are suitable as a basis for our Australian parakeets;
• an egg food. This also need not be self-manufactured. The commercially available preparations are, in general, of good quality. This part of the diet is to ensure that your birds get the necessary animal proteins.
• fruit and greens. These provide vitamins and minerals and can include garden fruit and vegetables plus grass and herbs from the wild;
• fresh twigs; these not only contain nutrients, but help relieve boredom and help keep the beak in good shape. Willow twigs are particularly useful.
• gravel; to help grind up food in the stomach.
• grit; to provide calcium.
• bathing and drinking water.

The fancier often can use imagination when feeding his birds. Various food sources in the wild, in the garden, and from fruit trees are available. Do not collect greens that are close to highways as vehicle exhaust fumes can pollute them. Also beware of plants that may be tainted by animal droppings, or by chemicals (herbicides, insecticides, fungicides).

The more varied the bird's diet the better and, if the diet is thoughtfully provided, there will be no need for all kinds of artificial vitamin/mineral preparations; all that is required will be in the diet itself. Do not overfeed and remember that "enough is as good as a feast."

The importance of variety was brought home to me in a year-long study in Australia on the feeding habits of the rosella. Feeding on grasses, herbs, shrubs, and trees, these birds made use of 82 species!

Australian parakeets are thus mainly herbivorous, feeding largely on plant material. The small

Feeding and Food

amount of animal proteins required are obtained from insects and other small invertebrates consumed accidentally while taking plant food or sometimes deliberately.

In addition to the normal seed ration, parakeets can be given germinated seed. The required amount of seed is soaked in water for 24 hours. Then it is rinsed thoroughly in clean water, drained, and placed in a dish in a warm place. Depending on the temperature, the seed will begin to germinate in two or three days. During this process it is a good idea to rinse the seed again to help minimize the risk of mold forming. The nutritive value is best when the shoots are $3/32$ to $1/8$ inch (2–3 mm) long.

In the winter, give parakeets more oily seeds (sunflower seeds, for example). This will help them resist the colder temperatures.

In frosty weather, the drinking water is likely to freeze over so this must be replaced frequently. Birds soon find out that they can eat snow and thus quench their thirst. You also can break up the ice in the dish or scrape a layer off; the birds will like to nibble on a piece of ice. In my aviaries I regularly see birds holding a piece of ice in the foot. Sometimes a bird will throw the drinking vessel about in play. This can be stopped by weighing it down with a heavy stone or brick, or fastening it somehow to a surface.

Giving charcoal when a bird has diarrhea is a waste of time. Charcoal is not digested and because it is porous it can remove valuable nutrients from the bird's digestive tract when it leaves the body.

Rearing Food

As far as feeding goes, the most crucial part of a parakeet's life is the first four or five weeks. Most seedeaters are altricial (hatching at a relatively early stage of development) and no longer receive the balanced diet of the egg yolk during the critical fast growth stage. Thus, during this time of growth and development of body and plumage it is essential for the hatchlings to receive a diverse and nutritive diet. Australian parakeets, like most seedeaters when rearing young, will forage for insects and other invertebrates as well as the usual seeds, buds, fruits, nuts, and so on to make a diet much more varied than they are likely to receive in captivity. However, there are a number of brands of excellent commercial rearing food available that will provide growing birds with an optimum diet. Canary breeders have a particularly good choice of rearing foods that, fortunately, also are very suitable for cockatiels and other Australian parakeets. In fact, similar amounts of proteins, starches/sugars, fats, vitamins, and minerals are required by all growing birds. Rearing foods containing adequate amounts of each of these dietary constituents will therefore normally result in healthy youngsters. However, some of these rearing foods may contain by-products that are not liked by the birds. It may therefore be necessary to provide a choice of two or three brands to ensure that your birds are getting sufficient quantities.

Concentrated or Universal Food

Various brands of concentrated bird foods are available on the market. These can be very useful to provide regular tonics for your birds, providing only scientifically prepared and tested well-known brands are offered. Concentrated foods contain nutrients that may be absent from the average seed mixture. For example, most commercially available seed mixtures will be deficient or low in amino acids (arginine, lysine, and methionine), choline, riboflavin and provitamin A. Seeds do not contain vitamin D_3 but it will be present in the animal product ingredient of the concentrated food. It is recommended that small quantities (concentrated foods can sour quickly in warm weather, so take care) of concentrated food are given daily to your birds throughout the year and not just in the breeding and molting seasons.

Feeding and Food

Fruit

Ensure that your birds always have a supply of fruit of one sort or another. Banana or orange is the favorite, but you also can try raisins, apples, pears, currants, strawberries, apricots, fresh pineapples, blackberries, mulberries, loganberries, lemons, dates, raspberries, grapefruits, juniper berries, cranberries, cherries, blueberries, kiwi fruit, gooseberries, rowan berries, mandarins, melons, peaches, plums, rose hips, hawthorn berries, wild elderberries, and figs. Remember the juice of some of these could stain the birds plumage if given in too great quantities. Too much also can cause loose droppings, so although you may give a variety of fruits, keep the daily quantities fairly low.

Beware of some fruits, such as the berries of the dwarf elder *(Sambucus ebulus)*, that are poisonous. Other poisonous plants include laburnum (especially the seeds), yew, the bark of silver birch *(Betula pendula)*, ivy, and black and fly honeysuckle *(Lonicera nigra* and *L. xylosteum)* which never should be offered to your birds. However, the wild honeysuckle *(L. periclymenum)* is enjoyed by most parakeets.

Insects

Australian parakeets also will use insects to gain animal protein in the diet—especially when young are being reared. Many adult parakeets also are partial to any fly, spider, caterpillar, or such that they can overpower. Suitable insects (and other invertebrate) foods include ants' "eggs" (really pupae), spiders, flies, crickets, grasshoppers, beetles, wax moths, tubifex and daphnia (the latter two are aquatic creatures that can be purchased in dried form, primarily as fish food, often compressed into blocks and very useful for your parakeets to gnaw at).

Table Scraps

Although it is important that your birds get a varied and balanced diet, in most cases this should not include scraps from the table. Starches and fats contained in some foods, such as potatoes ands butter, are not suitable foods. Candies, biscuits, and cakes also should be kept out of reach and the habit of allowing your tame parakeet to "eat at the table" should be discouraged (see also page 32).

Bird Pellets

It is impossible to give your captive birds the type and the variety of food they would find in their native habitats. The menu of aviary birds therefore must be as high as possible in variety and quality. The increasing popularity of keeping pet birds in the past decade or so has led to a growth in the pet animal food industry, resulting in all kinds of products on the market. Some of these are "pelleted and extruded diets for pet birds." These easy-to-feed diets are given in containers as one would give seed. They contain all of the dietary constituents in correct quantities and, in theory, other than water, all a bird requires to keep it in the best of health. However, it will be difficult to convert a bird that has been eating seed all of its life to take these diets! The best way to do it would be to give a mixture of seed and pellets or an extruded diet, gradually increasing the latter and decreasing the seed over a couple of weeks. Personally I think pelleted and extruded diets can be a bit monotonous for captive

Top and bottom left: Pennants or crimson rosellas are ▶ very sociable birds and a familiar sight in camps and national parks. They make excellent pets. Bottom right: The yellow rosella often is regarded as a form of the same species as the crimson.

birds and still would give seeds, fruit and green food as well. According to a 1990 survey by the American Pet Products Manufacturers Association, only 6 percent of all bird fanciers buy single-particle diets, whereas 70 percent of all bird owners rely on seed as the mainstay of their birds' diet!

Hygiene and Cleanliness

Hygiene and cleanliness go hand in hand; without the latter you won't get the former! Good hygiene prevents the spread of disease among captive stock. Utensils should be cleaned daily, preferably in the morning. Empty hulls should be blown off the seed before topping up the containers. Many beginners often make the mistake of putting new seed on top of empty hulls and eventually ending up with a dish of hulls only. Personally, I like to spread all the seed out daily on a sheet of newspaper, then blow the hulls away. The new seed is then put in the dish first and the remainder from previous days put on top of it. This way the bottom layer of seed never can get old gradually or form a breeding ground for bacteria or other pests.

Food and water vessels must be cleaned thoroughly at regular intervals, preferably not less than once per week. A solution of household bleach and water (1:1) makes an excellent disinfectant (leave the utensils soaking for 15 minutes) providing the utensils are rinsed thoroughly in clean water afterwards. Do not use seed containers unless they are dried out thoroughly. Damp seeds soon will turn sour, will mold, and will become infected with bacteria and other organisms possibly dangerous to our birds' health.

Some bird keepers believe that sick birds don't require food or water. This, of course, is nonsense! Indeed, give a bird its favorite food and try to get it to eat. Once eating and drinking with obvious appetite, the bird is on its way to recovery. Remember that a bird in a heated hospital cage will become very thirsty, and to prevent dehydration it must have clean, fresh water (with glucose, see page 53) all the time. Moreover, the water can be used as an aid to administering medicines and tonics.

◀ One of the best known Australian parakeets is the fast flying, brilliantly colored Eastern rosella; it often visits suburban gardens. These rosellas nest in any available hollow, and the females incubate up to nine eggs for some 20 days.

Breeding Australian Parakeets

Introduction

Individual breeding requirements may be found in The Species chapter. General points, including hand rearing, will be discussed here.

Australian parakeet breeding has developed into a fine art over the last few years. It generally is accepted that several species have been saved from extinction by intensive captive breeding. Amazingly, there are more captive specimens of some species than there are in the wild!

We can conclude from this that breeding parakeets successfully is not difficult. This does not mean that we will achieve equal successes with each species, but if you follow the tips given here, we are convinced your birds will reproduce regularly. Although Australian parakeets may be tops in popularity, they can, at the same time, give the greatest problems. However, if you own a good pair, then our Australian parakeets also will reward you. It is important to keep a close eye on the birds so that you know precisely what they require at all times. This is especially true of food and nest boxes. It also is important to keep each pair separate. Never set two or more pairs together in the same aviary (except in those situations cited in the text); this will lead to fighting among the males, infertile eggs, and similar problems. Pairs of the same species also should not be placed next to each other in adjacent aviaries; it is much better for the birds to have different species as direct neighbors. Always be aware of which species can be crossed with another. Some birds, even from different genera, may take an interest in each other in captive conditions and interspecific crossings are not unusual; for example the red-winged parakeet *(Aprosmictus erythropterus)* will cross readily with the Rock pebbler parakeet *(Polytelis anthopeplus)*. One should watch out for such cases. It is understandable, therefore, that birds that are "closely-related" should be housed as far removed from each other as possible. To sum up: never place birds of the same species next to each other in aviaries and keep birds of the same genus or closely-related species as far away from each other as possible.

The most difficult time for the parakeet fancier comes with the start of the breeding season. At this time there is much to experience; the birds wake up as though they have just come out of hibernation, and they throw themselves into all kinds of activities. The fancier must now consider increasing the protein in the birds' diets, providing nest boxes, and ensuring peace and quiet.

Photoperiod and temperature have a major influence on bringing birds into breeding condition. In nature there is an important breeding stimulus in the sudden abundance of food combined with optimum weather conditions. In Australia, therefore, the start of the breeding season is strongly influenced by the rainy seasons. The eggs usually are laid two to three weeks after the first rainfalls of the season. The nearer to the equator the birds' habitat, the less they react to changes in the photoperiod. This is explained by the fact that in the tropics lengths of days and nights are similar all year; therefore the availability of food becomes a more important factor.

Against this background, it is no coincidence that some of the most successful aviary birds (budgerigars, zebra finches, cockatiels) all come from the same environment; they feed mainly on grass seeds and breed after the start of the rains, whenever there is an abundance of seed. In this context, they can breed here, at any time of the year.

The lack of influence of the photoperiod can be seen, for example, in the hooded parakeet and in Brown's rosella—birds that come from the extreme tropical north of Australia. They breed there in the wet season and do the same here, sometimes breeding in September. In recent years, there also are pairs that breed in our spring.

Australian parakeets are, in general, not particularly affectionate towards each other, and one rarely sees them sitting close to each other on a perch; there almost always is a space between them. This cautious behavior must be changed when the breeding season starts. The cock must endeavor to approach the hen. In this group of parakeets, it is achieved by the development of a courtship ceremony in which he must gradually approach her in a cautious manner. His behavior will stimulate her breeding instincts and he becomes so completely wrapped up in his behavior that he slowly loses his fears.

The repertoire of movements is rather limited. He can jump up and down, bend and stretch, turn his head from left to right, shimmer his wings, allow his wings to hang or to draw them up, twist his body, blink his eyes or enlarge his pupils. Not all movements are gentle towards the hen; some can be quite aggressive, for example the jump into the air. Although this may attract the attention of the hen, it also seems to be a warning to other cocks that the hen is no longer available.

Each species has developed its own courtship procedures, some of which are unique. Natural selection can enhance the effect by providing the performing parts of the body with increased color. A conspicuous color pattern in a particular spot will therefore give us clues to the kind of courtship of each species; a good example is the red-winged parakeet.

Cocks that nod or turn the head usually have strong colors there; those that let their wings hang usually have brightly colored wing feathers and those that raise the wings often have brighter colors below.

Keep the area around the aviaries as quiet as possible during the breeding season. Dogs and cats (are there bird fanciers who also have cats?) should be kept away, though birds can get used to a quiet domestic dog. You also must keep yourself in check, especially during routine inspections when you must keep all disturbances to the absolute minimum as some birds will leave their eggs at the slightest excuse. Feed and water your birds at set times so that they become accustomed to seeing you at those times and will accept you without fear, especially if you announce your approach with a whistle or a song. It is amazing what calming effect this has on aviary birds.

Breeding Opportunities

You already will know that most psittacines do not use nest material to build a nest. Exceptions to the rule are the Quaker parakeet of South America and the lovebirds of Africa and Madagascar. You must provide your Australian parakeets with a cavity in which they can nest. Most species breed in hollow trunks or limbs, making a nest cup in the wood pulp, splinters, or remains of other abandoned birds' nests at the base of the hollow. Being excellent gnawers, parakeets often enlarge the cavity to suit themselves and the chips fall to the floor of the hollow making an ideal bed for the eggs. In captivity you can use nest boxes or, if you can obtain them, hollow logs of the right dimensions. Give each pair of birds a choice of at least two different kinds of nest boxes so that they can decide themselves and do not, as it were, have to make do with what the fancier thinks is the right one. We personally have had the greatest successes by offering four nest boxes (of two different types), two types inside the shelter and two types in the flight. If the birds show no interest in a nest box within, say, ten days (you can see this as the birds do not even inspect the boxes), then we can move the boxes to another wall. You probably will wonder: why not hang a box on each wall in the first place? The answer to this is simple: it is not possible to tell in advance what sort of nest box the birds will accept. Thus if you hang the boxes on one wall and get no results, move them to the opposite wall and the birds still have a choice. Of course, wherever the boxes are affixed you must ensure that it is possible to inspect them with minimum disturbance to the birds. Once you know the type of nest box preferred by a particular pair, you can offer the same (or similar) box the following year.

But you must first know the type of nest boxes preferred by the parakeets. It can happen that a

Breeding Australian Parakeets

Various nest boxes. Top left clockwise: two closed nest boxes for small parakeet species; half-open nest box for finches; log nest for medium and large parakeets; grandfather clock nest box for large parakeets; and closed nest box with a removable concave bottom.

newly acquired pair will refuse to breed because they do not have an optimum diet or that they have (to them) an unsuitable nest box. If you happen to purchase a pair of "excitable" birds (birds that are too nervous), you must treat them with great patience (of course, if you have come to an arrangement with the supplier you may be able to exchange them for another pair or even get your money back). If the birds are still young and inexperienced, we sometimes can get results by changing the cocks around; this sometimes leads to excellent breeding pairs. Typically, the more robust species, after years of not breeding, will suddenly settle down and breed with excellent results if partners are changed.

All Australian parakeets breed in hollows. In the wild most of them seek a hollow limb or trunk, usually of a eucalyptus or gum tree. This is because such trees often are hard on the outside and soft in the middle (having been colonized at some stage by termites that digest the timber and convert it into a softer, honeycomb-like substance that is relatively easy to gnaw). Nest entrances are often where a rotten or termite infested branch has broken from a larger branch or the main trunk, leaving an exposed area that can be tunneled relatively easily.

Some species, for example the golden-shouldered and hooded parakeets, breed in termite mines, into which they tunnel when the mounds are softened in the rainy season. In captivity, these species will use a nest box as a substitute (see page 123).

It would be difficult to provide a natural nest cavity for captive parakeets. There are two possibilities: a natural, hollowed out branch of sufficient diameter, or a self-made nest box made of boards or plywood. The latter has several advantages:
• as Australian parakeets have been bred in them for generations, they normally are accepted;
• they are lighter in weight;
• you can make them exactly to your pattern and usually can arrange a more convenient inspection hatch.

What dimensions must a nest box have? You can follow a general rule. Each side of the square bottom of the box is the same length as the distance from beak to vent of the bird in question. Thus, each is almost the length of the bird minus its tail. The height of the box must be three times this amount. As this does not apply to all parakeets, especially the king parakeet, it is best to follow the species recommendations.

Nest boxes frequently are fashioned too large. The smaller they are, the easier it is for the bird to keep the inside warm. Even in the wild, birds sometimes nest in amazingly small holes in which the young have to sit on top of each other. This is not so bad when the interior walls are rough, as the upper nestlings can cling to the walls. In smaller nest boxes, the youngsters are forced to sit close to each other and keep each other warm. Another disadvantage of too large a nest box is that it will let in too much light; this may deter the bird from brooding. Most parakeets prefer to sit in the dark. In general, the entrance hole must be just wide enough to allow the bird entry. On one hand, this gives a better feeling of security; on the other hand, not too much light enters. This is not a hard and fast rule: in Australia parakeets sometimes will use larger nest cavities, especially when nothing else is available.

With self-made nest boxes, the entrance hole can be made in the center or to one side. The advantage of placing it on the side is that the light that enters is distributed irregularly and the hen can sit in the darkest corner. The hole need not necessarily be round; other shapes are permissible.

As the walls of nest boxes usually are smooth, it is a good idea to affix a piece of wire mesh inside to form a ladder, but make sure there are no loose ends in which a bird could get caught by its nails or leg band. It is perhaps better to knock a couple of large nails into one wall, or affix a couple of pieces of wood, but these may quickly be gnawed away. Affix a small perch near the entrance hole so that the hen has easy access to the box.

The nest box can be hung in various places, inside or out. I prefer inside, for the following reasons:
• It is relatively quieter; the chances of disturbance are minimized.
• At night no unpleasant things can cause the bird to panic and leave the nest.
• The box is protected from adverse weather conditions, such as late frosts, harsh sunlight, or driving rains.
• Inspection is much easier.

If you have a row of night shelters connected by a service passage at the rear, you can best hang the nest boxes on the walls adjoining the passage. You then can make little inspection hatches into the nest boxes from the passage side, so that you disturb as little as possible by inspections, but don't open it when the hen is sitting.

If you decide to place a nest box outside, see that it is reasonably protected from driving rain and strong sunlight; if part of the flight is covered, the box is best placed there.

With new birds that have not chosen a nest box

it is best to provide a choice of at least two nest boxes. In general, Australian parakeets that have been bred for many generations in captivity are not all that choosy about nest boxes. In this case you can, with the easier species, hang up a box where you think it should go. Watch carefully and if they don't go to nest in the breeding season, hang up another (preferably of a different type) in a different place. When you buy youngsters from a breeder, it also is advisable to see what type of nest box they were raised in, especially as the hen that often will choose a box similar to its own nursery.

Nest boxes can be left in the aviary all year round or they can be removed after the breeding season. Both methods have advantages and disadvantages. Boxes left hanging all year (which must of course be cleaned after the breeding season) allow the birds to decide when to go to nest as they would in the wild. A disadvantage of this is the risk of too low temperatures and night frosts. This can cause egg binding and other problems. Beware particularly of some species that have become almost domesticated and are barely influenced by the seasons (kakarikis, cockatiels, and some *Neophema* species for example).

With such birds it is best to remove the nest box, or block the entrance outside the breeding season. If the birds should accidentally get in the box at the wrong time and start laying eggs, allow the complete clutch to be laid, remove it, and *then* close off the entrance or take the box away.

Most fanciers provide their birds with nest boxes during March. Some are pedantic enough to have a set date on which they set them out, but this is not particularly necessary. The correct time is when the weather is right and the birds are ready. March may even be a bit too late for some species; the blue bonnet, for example, frequently goes to nest in late February if given the chance. Hanging boxes up too late occasionally can mean a lost breeding season, but an advantage here is that the risks of egg binding and other cold-induced conditions are minimized.

Breeding Australian Parakeets

There are several possibilities with regard to nesting materials. Though parakeets do not build a nest as such, it is a good idea to have a suitable base on which the eggs can be laid, rather than on bare wood: woodland soil mixed with rotting leaves, an upturned turf into which some sawdust has been pressed with the fist, rotten wood that the birds can themselves reduce by gnawing, wood shavings and so on. Do not use peat, fine sawdust, or other fine material, because this can cause respiratory problems in the youngsters—even aspergillosis—and the nostrils also can become blocked. Slightly moisten the nest material before it is added to the nest boxes; this will be of benefit to the development of the eggs.

Eggs

As soon as the birds have accepted a nest box, courtship and mating will follow and the first egg will be laid soon after. The number of eggs varies from species to species; they are white in color, having no need for camouflage in their dark hollows. Eggs are laid mostly in the afternoon or early evening every other day (thus about 48 hours between each egg). As incubation is started after the second or third egg is laid, the first youngsters hatch together, the rest in similar periods thereafter. Some breeders take the first egg out and replace it later in order to synchronize the hatchings as closely as possible. This really is not essential; in the wild there is a difference in age and size among a clutch and there is enough food for all. In very large clutches there can be a significant difference in age, in which case the youngest may be somewhat neglected.

If you remove eggs, do not forget that they have to be turned at regular intervals. Research has shown that a hen turns her eggs roughly every half hour during the day and every one to two hours at night, thus about 30 times per day. Turning prevents the embryo from adhering to the albumin or to the shell, which usually results in death. Eggs must not be stored at too high temperatures, otherwise the embryo will start to develop.

Eggs can be marked for identification with a soft lead pencil, but do not use ink or a felt pen, which can be poisonous. With all Australian parakeets except the cockatiel (in which cock and hen relieve each other—this shows a relation to the cockatoos, which do the same), the hen incubates and broods alone.

Eggs five or more days old can be inspected for fertility by candling. This involves holding the egg over a hole in an opaque sheet (a black card, for example) and shining a light through it from the rear. A special candling box in which the light bulb is totally enclosed can be used. A fertilized egg will show red blood vessels spreading from the darker embryonic shadow. Infertile eggs are translucent. Do not dispose of apparently infertile eggs immediately; the hen may not have started seriously brooding as early as you thought. An infertile egg also can have a function in the nest; it can hold heat for the benefit of the fertile eggs.

Infertile eggs can arise from various factors, such as infertile birds, inadequate diet, too young breeders that are not sexually mature, too aggressive a cock, and so on.

An egg with even a minute crack or dent will desiccate and the embryo will die. However we can reduce casualties by smearing clear nail polish over the defect, thus making it water tight again and helping out if the defect has not been in existence for too long. Use nail polish on as small an area of the shell as possible, otherwise respiration will be affected.

There is little point in opening an egg that seems to be taking too long to hatch. If the embryo is still alive, it usually will succumb to the trauma and die and in most cases it already will be dead.

Some birds are egg eaters. One cannot do much about this, other than remove each egg as soon as it is laid and replace it with an artificial one. Or give them a bad egg or one that you have filled with

Breeding Australian Parakeets

mustard, pepper, and the like. Hopefully the shocking taste will cure the bird of its bad habit. Should the hen start to incubate seriously, you must choose the right moment to return the original eggs. Eggs that, for one reason or another, are not incubated by the hen can be stored for a few days. Tests with cockatiels have shown that eggs are still viable after three days, but begin to deteriorate at six days. It is better to place eggs in an incubator after three to four days. What then happens depends on various things.

It is best to place the eggs as soon as possible under their original hen. If this is not possible, try to find suitable foster parents. These must be breeding at about the same time and the nearer related species it is the better. Difference in size also must not be too great. The last possibility is to allow the eggs to hatch in the incubator and attempt to hand rear the hatchlings (see page 49).

All in all, there is really nothing better than natural, parent-reared young. The parents can supply their young, in feeding and behavior, with what we are not capable of giving.

It is not that each egg must be separately fertilized. Birds copulate frequently, to increase the chances of fertilizing each egg. The male sex cells (spermatozoa) stay in the female body and remain fertile for several days, sometimes weeks. Even if the cock, for some reason or another is no longer present, the whole clutch of eggs still can be fertile. Such was the case of a pair of king parakeets in which the cock became so aggressive towards the hen after she laid the first egg that he had to be taken away by the owner. She laid another four eggs and from the total, the last four were fertile!

The incubation times are given in the Species chapter. There is a great variation in times. The climate can influence the time by one or two days in either direction.

Many eggs are lost because the nest box is too dry, so that the young cannot hatch properly and they die from suffocation. To prevent this, we can place a layer of damp peat at the bottom of the nest; over this we place a layer of wood shavings or other materials as mentioned at the beginning of this chapter. You will see that humidity is of great importance to the well-being of a clutch. Unfortunately, it sometimes occurs that (a point raised by Dr. H. D. Groen in his excellent book, *Australian Parakeets*) parakeets will throw all of the nest material out of the box, so that the eggs end up on a bone dry wooden bottom! For some species this does not matter so much, but in most cases the eggs will be lost. We have discussed the nest humidity requirements of the various species on pages 47–48. To prevent eggs being lost when nest material is thrown out, we can use nest boxes with a double floor; the upper floor having a few holes bored in it and a dish of water being placed between the two floors. Or a layer of damp sod can be pressed tightly into the nest bottom; the first method is preferred to the second.

Nestlings

As most species begin to breed in March or April, the first young leave the nest in May through July. The time from the first egg to fledging averages about two months. For the first few days eggs are not incubated by the hen, but she then sits for about three weeks before the young hatch. The hatchlings stay in the nest for up to five weeks before they fledge.

Parakeets are altricial, which means that they must be cared for by their parents for some time before they become independent (this is the opposite to precocial, which means that the young can run, feed and even fly shortly after hatching—pheasants, for example). After hatching, the hen broods the young for a day or so because they are not yet capable of keeping themselves warm.

The weight of the newborn bird is about two thirds the weight of the egg before it hatched; the hatchling will still have the yolk sac attached to it, which will continue to provide it with nourishment for a day or so. The young are not fed in the first 24 hours. If you are breeding indoors under artificial light, you must ensure that the period of light is adequate. There must be time for the young to be fed adequately. However, it is not necessary to provide light for more than 14 hours per day. Do not turn all lights off at once—an incubating or brooding hen that is off the nest at that moment and suddenly is plunged into darkness will not find her way back to the nest and you may as well write the brood off. Try to have a nightlight (5–7 watts) burning all night long, or affix timers and dimmers to your system.

The young are ready for leg banding at about one week of age. This can be done in one of two ways: firstly, with two toes forward and two backward; secondly, add the longest of the rear toes to the front, thus three forward and the shortest pointing backwards. Although the ankle joint is made a little thicker in the latter method, it tends to be easier. The advantage is that the ring has only a short distance to go once past the ankle joint; in the first

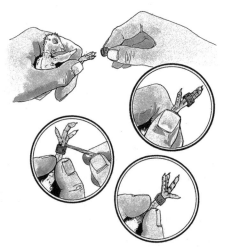

Banding a chick: preparing to slip the band on; the two front toes enclosed by the band; after you push the band down, the two back toes are pulled out with a toothpick; the band is in place.

method it must pass along the longer rear toe, which can be difficult especially if you are a little late in applying it.

When the ring is in position, see that it is not overloose; if so, inspect it regularly until the leg has grown sufficiently enough to prevent it from coming off. One excellent advantage of leg rings is that you can identify a bird without catching it. And if you have young from two pairs of the same species, those from one pair can be banded on the left leg, and on the right leg for the other pair. It is then easy to select unrelated pairs.

Under normal circumstances, the parent birds provide their young with all their needs—that is providing you have supplied an adequate diet, and so on. When the young first leave the nest box (fledging), they will be nervous and flighty. And this is no wonder—everything is new and unknown! When they enter the flight, it is possible that they will fly full tilt into the wire mesh as they cannot see it so well and do not know what it is. You can help prevent this by hanging a few twigs or some sacking in front of the wire before the young enter the flight. Also, ensure that youngsters have returned to the shelter at night; an encounter with a cat or an owl could have disastrous consequences.

The fledglings are fed by the parents for some time after fledging. They gradually learn to feed themselves and must therefore stay at least three weeks with the parents. As soon as the parents start persecuting their young, or start another brood, then they (the young) must be removed to separate accommodations.

Fledglings have the so-called juvenile plumage and they molt in the following autumn (the so-called first molt), whereby some species get their full adult plumage. This depends on the sexual maturity of the birds—the later a bird matures, the longer it will take to get its full adult plumage. A good first molt is important to prepare the bird for a long fall and winter.

Of course, not all breeding processes go without a hitch but we should not always put the blame on

the birds. Try to pinpoint what has gone wrong by answering the following questions:
• Have you bought best quality birds?
• Are these birds sexually mature?
• Have the birds had enough time to become accustomed to their new environment and to each other?
• Are they compatible?
• Do you definitely have a true pair?
• Have you supplied an adequate, balanced diet with an increased protein content for the breeding season?
• Are nesting facilities adequate?
• Did the birds come well through the last molt?
• Do the birds have related neighbors which may have put them through aggressive behavior?

If you find no clues to the lack of breeding success, be patient and allow your birds another breeding season. Do not be too hasty in buying another batch of birds. Not every pair will reproduce on command and that is a good thing, otherwise the fancy would lose its attraction.

Surrogate Incubation

Sometimes a particular hen will lay a clutch of eggs and then fail to incubate them. There can be many reasons for this—inadequate diet and/or accommodations being at the top of the list. Unfortunately, even in the most efficiently run aviaries, the occasional hen will refuse to incubate. In most cases the hen will start to incubate after laying the third egg. If the bird has not started to seriously incubate after the third (or sometimes the fourth) egg, then we have to do something about it if we do not want to lose the young. As soon as the clutch is complete and the hen refuses to sit, remove them carefully and store them in a cool place for one or two days. Although we would advise you to make or obtain a still air (not forced air) incubator, it is useless storing the eggs for a long period. Thus we should consider using foster parents.

You could put the eggs under an incubating bird, but this entails the risk of the double clutch being too large and you might end up with two lost clutches. An incubator is thus the only answer.

Foster Parents

Personally, I put the eggs in the incubator at the same time that another hen begins to incubate. After six days I candle the eggs from the incubator and those from the foster parents; all infertile eggs are discarded and replaced with good eggs from the incubator with the incubating hen. The eggs are not placed capriciously in the nest. I must keep an eye on the hen and see that she is attending the nest and being fed by the cock. It is possible for totally unrelated species to act as foster parents as long as the species are of similar size, but it is better to use related species if possible. Red-rumped parakeets make excellent foster parents and these birds often have raised a clutch consisting of four or more species! Other good foster parents include Bourke's parakeets (for smaller species, but also for red rumps) and all rosella species. Even budgerigars, cockatiels, and lovebirds can be used as foster parents for smaller species. Many breeders have special pairs of birds that they use exclusively as foster parents! And some of these never get to raise their own brood. In my experiences, the best results are achieved by birds that have never incubated and reared their own clutch (or have incubated at all). This is especially so with cockatiels. You must be prepared to accept that the chances of success or failure are 50/50, but these are risks you must take, like it or not!

Lovebirds, perhaps surprisingly, have shown themselves to be good foster parents to rosellas, Bourkes, elegants, turquoisines, and blue-winged grass parakeets. Budgerigars are suitable as foster parents only to turquoisine parakeets and we must reckon with even chances of success.

Artificial Incubation

I personally have always had the best results with a small still air incubator with a horizontal egg rack made of fine mesh upon which is laid a piece of burlap (to prevent the chicks' feet going through the mesh when they hatch and possibly breaking their legs). The incubator is heated by warm air that passes over the eggs and leaves via the ventilator opening(s). The temperature just above the eggs is 102° F (39° C). I have had the best results with a constant temperature of 103° F (39.5° C). A thermostat will maintain the constant temperature and a thermometer will ensure that the thermostat is holding the correct temperature. The thermometer should be placed just above the eggs, near one of the sides with the mercury bulb at the same level as the eggs. The incubator has insulated walls so that the constant heat is distributed evenly. The recommended thermostat is the so-called ether-capsule thermostat, which is very sensitive and exact; it is better than the sturdier but less sensitive bi-metal thermostat. Although many aviculturists prefer still air incubators with manual turning of eggs, other incubators of choice among breeders are those with moving air and automatic turning, the so-called forced air incubators. There are various makes and prices. The primary requirement of an incubator, whatever the make, should be that it has an efficient thermostat.

If you are not using an incubator with automatic turning, you must do it yourself. Twice a day is enough, perhaps once at 8 A.M. and again in the evening at about 9 P.M. Do not be afraid that opening the door of the incubator will cool the eggs too rapidly; they need the fresh air for their healthy development. When turning eggs (be careful not to break the shells) use a plastic spoon. Check the water level in the vessel below the egg rack; there always must be enough water in the vessel to guarantee humidity of approximately 68 percent around the developing eggs, preventing desiccation and enhancing development and problem-free hatching. Before placing water in the incubator, check the room's humidity, which frequently is higher than you might think, especially in states like Florida. The higher the humidity outside the incubator, the smaller the amount of water in the incubator reservoir. As proper humidity is crucial to the development of the egg, all breeders should use a hygrometer, an instrument for measuring the water vapor content of the atmosphere.

As soon as the eggs are pipped or are ready to hatch, they can be placed under a brooding bird; its own clutch is taken away from it. This may be discarded or we can place this in the incubator, creating, as it were, a brooding circle! If there are several incubating birds, the eggs can be distributed among these. We must keep records of what has been placed where, so that we know which is which later on. The incubator also can be used if a hen suddenly abandons a clutch (but give it a couple of hours first—parakeet eggs can take more than we may think).

It is advisable to weigh each hand-reared chick before and after each feeding. Always determine the fullness of the chick's crop and stop feeding immediately when food starts flowing back into the mouth.

Hand Rearing

Sometimes we do not have an available foster parent to incubate or to brood. In such cases it will be necessary to attempt hand rearing of the incubator hatched young. Chicks that have lost their parents for one reason or another also will require hand rearing.

The Brooder

Directly after the young have hatched they should be taken from the incubator and placed in a brooder. This is a glass-fronted wooden box, a hospital cage, or an old aquarium. It may be heated from above with a couple of 60 watt bulbs and the temperature maintained at 99.5° F (37.5° C) for the first couple of days. The temperature may be reduced gradually as the young increase in weight but do not allow it to drop to below 86° F (30° C) until they are ready to be acclimatized to lower temperatures. The brooder temperature should be controlled preferably with a thermostat because young birds are unable to tolerate sudden temperature changes. As the birds grow, they are able to move in and out of the heat source, thus choosing their own preferred temperature—this will do them no harm at all.

Feeding

Because excellent balanced rearing diets are available, there is little point in making your own. All of these come with instructions. Most formulas require just the addition of warm water (sterilized but not distilled). A plastic eye dropper or syringe can be used to administer the food or, like me, you may find a teaspoon with the sides bent in is more convenient.

Newly hatched parakeets are small and tender, and have tiny soft beaks. By gently tapping the beak with the utensil you often will encourage the nestling to gape (open its beak). If it refuses to gape, you will have to open the beak gently with a toothpick

Spoon feeding young chicks. Hand feeding also is done with a syringe.

or similar item. As soon as the beak is open, drop a tiny drop of water into the throat. The bird soon will get used to this and will open its beak voluntarily when you give it a gentle tap.

When to Feed: Newly hatched chicks rarely feed in the first 10–15 hours, thereafter start with a drop of lukewarm water. One hour later give it another drop containing some clean (pure white), powdered cuttlefish bone and natural yogurt. After another hour, give it another drop of the same and thereafter feed a few drops of highly diluted hand rearing diet every hour. Once each day, I mix in a little yogurt as this contains vitamin K, the blood clotting vitamin. This vitamin also can be found in some grains, soya meal, and so on, which usually is included in the rearing food, so the inclusion of yogurt is not absolutely necessary. Nevertheless, I like to give it to the birds as an additional supplement, even if it not the birds' favorite food.

An example of a typical feeding schedule for hand-reared nestlings, from day 4 to day 25 is as follows:

• Days 4–9: Feed every two hours, except between the hours of midnight and 5 AM. Prepare the food to the consistency of creamy milk.

Breeding Australian Parakeets

• Days 10–14: Give similar formula every three hours from 5 A.M. to midnight.

• Days 15–20: Prepare slightly thicker formula and feed every four hours. After 20 days, house birds in a cage with low perches and a shallow dish of water. Birds of this age will begin to experiment for themselves, so provide a few "snacks," such as well washed twigs of apple, hazel, plum, or willow cut into short lengths; crushed canary grass seed, powdered cuttlebone (clean and white), egg food, and millet spray. The latter should be scalded with boiling water to sterilize it.

• Days 21–25: Continue hand feeding with rearing mixture two to three times a day, but encourage birds to feed themselves by offering a free choice of sprouted seeds and millet spray (fresh and not scalded). Mix some dry formula with the sprouted seeds and also give finely chopped fruits and greens, and cuttlebone powder.

If you successfully hand rear a bird, it will become very tame and affectionate, as it will regard you as its parent. Such birds are the best to use if you want a tame pet and, perhaps surprisingly, they can turn out to be exceedingly good parents, bringing the strongest of offspring into the world.

Feeding Method: Warm water (100–110° F) (not distilled) or apple juice is added to the rearing mixture and mixed well until it has the consistancy of creamy milk. Never try to give too thick a mixture as it can compact in the bird's crop and cause a serious stoppage. If this problem occurs accidentally, it usually can be corrected by giving the bird lukewarm water and gently massaging the crop.

Place the nestling on a flat surface, preferably on a warm towel, and support it with one (warm!) hand, while feeding it with the other. The mixture can be administered from a syringe or plastic dropper, or let it roll off a bent-sided teaspoon. All feeding implements should be warmed to the temperature of the mixture before use. The temperature of the feeding mixture (100–110° F, but not higher to avoid "crop burn") can be maintained during feeding by placing the dish in a pan of warm water. If the bird won't open its beak, try stimulating it with a gentle tap—this generally will do the trick. Examine the bird's crop before each feeding to determine the frequency and quantity of feeding required. The crop should never become completely empty but it can empty itself in three to four hours. On the other hand, try not to overfill the crop as this could cause various complications, including asphyxiation. If the food starts flowing back into the mouth, stop feeding and give it a rest before trying again when the mouth is completely empty.

Feeding should be synchronized with swallowing. When the nestling swallows, accompanied by head bobbing, deliver the mixture quickly. Place the feeding device in the mouth, over the tongue. After each feeding, rinse the inside of the bird's mouth with a few drops of warm (100–110° F) water and clean its beak, head, and any other parts that may have become soiled, plus its vent; then return it to its warm brooder.

Keep separate feeding utensils and feeding dishes for each bird and do not go from one bird to the other with the same utensil. Always clean all feeding utensils after use and sterilize by immersing in boiling water.

The Sick Parakeet

Hopefully your birds never will become sick, but one should know about likely diseases and their treatment if an emergency arises. Although most Australian parakeets are very hardy once acclimatized to their new surroundings, they will quickly fall ill if proper care and nutrition are lacking. A great deal of consideration therefore should be given to providing our birds with the best possible housing, food, and other aspects of their care. By taking the time and trouble (and sometimes expense) of getting things right, you will be ready to avert any potential disasters.

The duration of sickness in a bird is usually quite short. If symptoms are not noticed in their early stages it may be too late to effect a complete cure and the bird may be lost. Familiarize yourself therefore with every bird and learn what constitutes their normal behavior. Then when there is any sudden change in behavior you will know there could be something requiring further investigation. For example: if a bird should suddenly start sitting in places it normally avoids, this could be a sign that the bird is sick. If it makes a bigger mess with its food than usual or sits around with its feathers puffed out and its eyes half shut, or has dirt around its vent, there is a good chance that the bird is sick.

First Aid

Sometimes there are only the merest of clues indicating that a bird is sick. Nevertheless don't hesitate to take appropriate action. Immediate action may save a lot of trouble, and lives of your birds later on. If you should be incorrect in your diagnosis, you will have lost nothing other than a little time. It is much better to be overcaring rather than nonchalant.

If you think one of your parakeets is sick, the first step is to isolate it from the other birds in the collection. It is possible that it is suffering with a communicable disease that poses a danger to all your birds. As soon as a bird has been diagnosed as having an infectious disease, the whole aviary,

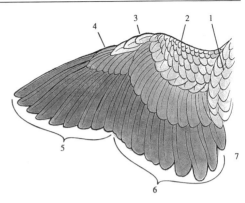

Knowing a bird's anatomy and the various parts of its plumage is useful not only for conversations with veterinarians, but also for describing different bird species. The wing:

1. Scapulars   2. Middle and lesser coverts
3. Spurious wing   4. Primary coverts
5. Primaries   6. Secondaries   7. Tertiaries

feeding utensils, perches, toys, and accessories should be disinfected (see following Commonly Used Disinfectants chart).

The sick bird is best placed in a special hospital cage, the back and sides of which are enclosed and only the front exposed. Add glucose and a multivitamin preparation or better still, a balanced electrolyte (Pedialyte, Gatorade, fruit juice) to the bird's favorite food (or drink), but be sure to follow the manufacturer's instructions. If a bird refuses to feed or drink for a period of 24 hours, you will have to force-feed it every hour or it will die of starvation even if the disease hasn't killed it by then. Give the bird lactose-free baby food with a spatula, about 3 cc per serving.

The hospital cage may have a thermostatically controlled heating element, otherwise you can use an infrared heating lamp in front of or suspended above the cage. By adjusting this up and down and having a thermometer in the cage you can arrive at a constant chosen temperature in the cage of 85–90° F (29–32° C). If necessary, cover the front of the cage with a cloth to help retain heat. The cage

The Sick Parakeet

Commonly Used Disinfectants

Available through grocery stores, pet stores, veterinarians, and janitorial supply houses.

Lysol   Manufactured by Lehn & Fials Products, Div. of Sterling Drug Inc.
Dilution: 4 ounces per gallon water.
All purpose disinfectant.

One-Stroke Environ   Manufactured by Vestal.
Dilution: ½ ounce per gallon water.
All-purpose disinfectant; official disinfectant of the USDA.

Clorox   Manufactured by the Clorox Co.
Dilution: 6 ounces per gallon water.
May be irritating to skin; may be corrosive to bare metal.
Excellent for concrete flooring.

Betadine   Manufactured by Purdue-Frederick, Inc.
Dilution: $3/4$ ounce per gallon water.
Excellent noncorrosive disinfectant, but more expensive.
Available through veterinarians.

Note: Always follow manufacturers' recommendations.

preferably should have a false mesh bottom so that the bird's droppings fall through and thus prevent the bird soiling itself or even reinfecting itself with its own feces.

Once the bird has recovered, the heat should be reduced *gradually* back to room temperature by moving the lamp a few inches further away at two-hour intervals and finally switching it off. Avoid damp or drafty conditions; we don't want the bird to catch a cold on top of its other problems.

Internal diseases often are very difficult to diagnose and for valuable birds it is worth the expense of employing a good avian veterinarian. If the bird should die, even after all your efforts, get your veterinarian to arrange an autopsy on the corpse and find the cause of death. Then, in the case of infectious diseases, timely prophylactic measures may be taken.

Hospital Cages

The serious breeder of Australian parakeets will ensure he has at least one hospital cage for use in emergency. The application of moist heat to sick birds is one of the major and most effective forms of treatment and a hospital cage is the best way to carry this out. You can buy ready-made hospital cages, but these usually are expensive. Should you find the price excessive, you can make a very serviceable model of your own at considerably less expense. The cage should be enclosed on all sides except the front, which has a sliding glass panel, and can be made of sheet metal or plywood. A good size is 28 inches high, 16 inches wide, and 20 inches deep (70 x 40 x 50 cm). Install four 60 watt bulbs so that these work independently of each other. This will enable you to maintain any desired temperature.

An easy to read thermometer is affixed to one wall of the cage. A sliding tray in the base of the tray will take a layer of dry sand, which will soak up the moisture from the bird's droppings. This should be replaced twice a day to remove sources of reinfection. In evaluating a sick bird, it is important to monitor daily its excretion. This can be done only if the substrate lends itself to that evaluation, hence use paper towels or something impervious to water both in the morning and late afternoon.

Above the tray, affix a mesh grid through which the bird's droppings can fall (see above). A small door at one end of the cage will be more convenient than removing the glass panel for servicing. Keep

The Sick Parakeet

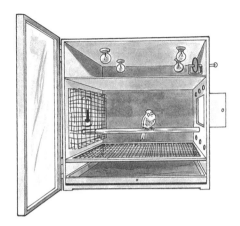

Hospital cage. Maintaining a relatively high temperature is essential for the proper and successful treatment of the patient.

an eye on the water supply at all times, as the high temperature will make the bird very thirsty and it normally will drink a lot.

Great caution must be taken in temperature control because a sick bird is already under stress, and too high or too low a temperature can kill it. When dealing with offspring of valuable birds, the cost of a professionally-made hospital cage will be earned back many times over in the course of its use.

A few ventilation holes should be drilled in the homemade hospital cage at each end of the box so that sick birds are well supplied with fresh air. The cage should be constructed in such a way that you have easy access to all parts of the interior. When the sick bird has recovered (or sadly, died in spite of your efforts) the hospital cage should be thoroughly scrubbed and disinfected, ready for another emergency.

What To Look For

The conscientious fancier continually will be on the lookout for signs of disease or parasites and it is wise to set aside a little time each week to specifi-

cally and thoroughly inspect the birds and their quarters. Anything found in its early stages usually can be dealt with more easily and will save a great deal of trouble later. When inspecting birds, blow some of their feathers to one side to look for parasites; you may have to use a magnifying glass. If the feathers should have a brush-like appearance take immediate action! (see page 63). A bird losing weight (if its breastbone sticks out, for example) or getting too obese, should be isolated for individual treatment (see page 65).

Colds and other respiratory infections are indicated by wet nostrils and labored, squeaky breathing. Aspergillosis causes gasping and a gaping beak. Check the eyes for inflamed edges; feel the legs and wings for signs of abnormalities. Look under the wings and examine the whole body surface for signs of cysts or tumors. Check the vent (cloacal opening) regularly for signs of diarrhea (you don't need to catch the bird to do this), indicating an intestinal problem. A hen bird looking distressed and with a swollen lower abdomen could well be suffering from egg binding.

Remember that a bird can starve to death in as little as one to two days. It is important that you get a sick bird to take some form of nutrition (and water) even if it means force-feeding it. Many birds die from starvation rather than the disease that made them lose their appetite (see also under glucose, page 39).

A bird that appears to have recovered completely from a disease should not be returned immediately to its normal quarters as it may still be capable of transmitting infection. Keep it in quarantine for a period and, at the same time, you gradually can acclimatize it back to normal temperatures.

Preventing Infections

The best way to control infectious diseases is with prophylactic care. Any person who has to care for sick birds is himself a potential carrier of the disease. Thus personal hygiene is also very important, especially with regard to washing the hands after each contact. I have been dismayed frequently by seeing bird keepers failing to follow this simple practice. For example, if one of your birds had coccidiosis or some other contagious disease and you handled it and the next one without washing your hands, you would be a great help in infecting the whole stock!

You therefore must be highly meticulous both with yourself and with your birds. Even when rubber gloves are worn to handle a sick bird, they must be disinfected before being used again. You must also take great care not to reuse any item (food, utensil, perch, cuttlefish bone, and so on) from a sick bird's cage or aviary unless it has been sterilized thoroughly and, if disposable, it should be preferably incinerated.

The avoidance of stress in captive birds is also one of the major factors in disease prevention. Birds kept in optimum conditions will have the highest amount of resistance and their bodies will be able to overcome any disease organisms that try to invade. However, a bird that recently has been caught from the wild or has had a change of accommodations, possibly a change of climate, will be scared and confused, thus stressed. You can make this stress even worse by putting the bird in a damp, drafty cage and letting the dog bark at it all day. This bird will be so stressed that its natural resistance will completely fail and it will be open to all kinds of disease organisms.

Diseases and Injuries

Sickness in a bird may be divided into three major categories:
• Contagious diseases (those that are caused by living organisms and can be passed from one bird to another).
• Noncontagious diseases (abnormalities caused by inadequate diet, e.g., malnutrition or avitaminosis).

• Mechanical injuries (wounds caused by mechanical or environmental effects, e.g., broken leg, frostbite).

The following alphabetical list includes all three categories:

Aspergillosis

This is a very unpleasant fungus infection of the air passages. It is caught by breathing in the spores of the fungus *Aspergillus fumigatus*. The source of aspergillosis spores is in moldy bread, seeds, chaff, musty hay, straw, and similar items; certain plants such as those belonging to the genus *Asperula* also may be a source of infection. The spores germinate in the lungs and air sacs, producing toxic substances that damage the tissues lining the respiratory system. An accumulation of yellow, cheese-like pus develops, interfering with the respiration and often causing a rasping breath and a panting, gaping demeanor. The bird loses its appetite, weakening it even further. No home cure so far has proven successful. However, your avian veterinarian may be able to help. Recent good results (over 70 percent success) have been achieved using ketoconazal per os, over one month. For lung and air sac aspergillosis, ultrasonore misting with miconade fluorocycine or amphoteracine-B might be helpful.

To prevent this unpleasant disease never give old or moldy seeds. Do not give spilled seed a chance to become moldy. Clean the aviary frequently and regularly, sweeping up all spilled food. Try to prevent dust and plant spores blowing into the aviary, particularly if you live near a lumber yard, or where straw or hay is stored (damp straw and hay is particularly dangerous). If a bird is

Top left: Golden-mantled or Eastern rosellas are ready ▶ to start a family during their second year. Top right: Blue-cheeked or pale-headed rosellas live in woodland, savanna, and lightly wooded farmland, and often are seen with red-winged and ringneck parakeets. Below: A pair of Brown's or Northern rosellas.

infected, the whole aviary must be inspected and cleaned. Try to find the source of infection and eliminate it. Use a 1 percent solution of copper sulphate solution as a (fungicide) disinfectant. Give birds exposed to infection a good multvitamin preparation, high in vitamin A.

Coccidiosis

Coccidiosis is caused by microscopic protozoan parasites, which fortunately occur only infrequently in Australian parakeets. The coccidia, which mature in the intestines, are spread by the droppings of infected birds being consumed (accidentally or deliberately) by healthy birds. Birds could be affected for a long time before the disease is diagnosed. However, consult an avian veterinarian if you notice a gradually decreased appetite, typically coupled with weight loss and watery droppings that may contain some blood. Such symptoms could indicate a case of coccidiosis. Sulfa drugs may help cure the disease in its earlier stages. Good hygiene is the only sure method of prevention.

Colds

The term "colds" can be used to describe all manner of respiratory infections. Stress brought on by low temperatures, drafts, and dampness, or a vitamin A deficiency, can make the bird lose its immunity to various bacteria, viruses, or fungi. A bird suffering from a disease of the respiratory tract usually will be fighting for its breath, panting and gasping, often coupled with a wheezing sound. It will gape and its tail will move up and down. The bird is likely to sneeze and cough, have a runny nose, and probably will stop eating. In most cases it will sit moping in a corner with its plumage puffed

◀ Top: A pair of Barnard's or Mallee ringneck parakeets. In the wild, these impressive birds usually are seen in pairs or small flocks in the company of pale-headed rosellas. Below: The subspecies of the Barnard's parakeet is the Cloncurry—a very popular aviary bird, more so than the nominate form!

out. Such a bird requires instant attention—preferably isolated in a hospital cage. Clean its nostrils by dabbing with a cotton ball and use a mist sprayer to spray a fine, warm mist of water into the cage to help moisturize the inflamed lining of the respiratory tract (a standard vaporizer available at your drugstore can be used). Consult an avian veterinarian and check to see that your birds are being kept in optimum conditions.

Diarrhea

Diarrhea is the symptom of a number of intestinal upsets that can occur in Australian parakeets. The simplest form of diarrhea is caused by too much green food or fruit or protein, especially to birds that are not used to it. This is easily adjusted, just cut down on causative food. A more serious form of diarrhea can be caused by bad food, which is tainted or spoiled to the extent that it contains toxins; perhaps DDT, lindane, or other insecticides. Always ensure that your birds get only the best! Diarrhea also can be caused by poorly ventilated quarters in warm weather, or by cold drafty conditions. Extremes in temperature, especially sudden changes, are a threat to the health of the birds. The worst forms of diarrhea are caused by infections of the body—especially of the intestines.

Visible signs of impaired intestinal function include the diarrhea itself (watery, often abnormally colored and foul smelling droppings; a wetness around the vent), listlessness, hunching, and fluffing. In serious cases the bird will leave its perch and take to some corner of the floor, often with its head tucked under its wing. The bird may drink a lot, but usually will refuse to eat.

Such cases are best referred to an avian veterinarian, but there are some remedies you can try. I personally have had some success with chamomile tea. You can give the patient boiled rice, oat flakes, and millet spray. You can give rice water instead of the usual drinking water, or you can use a commercial preperation called Norit, a tablet of which is dissolved in a tablespoon of water. Then give the patient one or two drops in the beak using an eye dropper or a similar method.

As is usual, the sick bird should be placed in a warmed hospital cage and maintained at about 90° F (32° C). Quiet and warmth, coupled with the prescribed treatment, will help the patient recover.

A poisoned bird also should be kept warm and given fresh green food and drinking water in which a little bicarbonate of soda has been dissolved (about .035 ounce (1 g) per full glass of water). Other good purges include fresh milk or a few drops of Pepto-Bismol. Never provide bicarbonate of soda for more than three days running. Overindulgence in high protein foods such as egg or soft foods, especially in the breeding season, can bring on a special type of poisoning. A fancier may forget or be ignorant of the fact that egg food is a *supplement* to the birds' normal diet and not a diet on its own. Affected birds suddenly will show all the typical symptoms of poisoning. They will be dull and lethargic, have respiratory problems, and will stop flying. Often they may have severe diarrhea, which can lead to a quick death.

A case of diarrhea is not always necessarily dangerous. If it appears with no other symptoms it may be simply a case of indigestion or too much of a certain food. But to be on the safe side, it is always best to have the bird examined by an avian veterinarian.

E. coli Infections

Escherichia coli are gram-negative bacteria, usually referred to simply as *E. coli*, that can cause infections in human beings as well as Australian parakeets. Some people think that *E. coli* are normal inhabitants of a bird's intestine, but this definitely is not the case, and if they spread to the lungs, liver, and heart they soon can be fatal. The best preventive measure is good hygiene. Wash your hands before you handle birds, prepare feed, inspect nests, or indeed any activity involving your birds. Prevent fecal contamination and on no account use spoiled food. Give fresh water daily and more often if

necessary. Keep perches, nest boxes, and all parts of cages and aviaries clean and do not allow droppings to accumulate. It is also very important that periodic cultures be performed by your avian veterinarian to screen birds for potential pathogen.

Treatment for an *E. coli* infection consists of three to four drops of Kaopectate or Pepto-Bismol, every four hours. Such preparations will coat the digestive tract, soothing the inflammation. If improvement does not occur within 24 hours, seek the advice of an avian veterinarian who may prescribe use of one of the many antibiotics (i.e. amoxicillin, or a *Lactobacillus* preparation) that can provide relief. (Lactobacillus preparations are excellent as they replace helpful intestinal bacteria that are lost when birds are medicated with antibiotics. Thus, although they do not cure any illness, they do help to ameliorate them.)

Egg Binding

This is a case of a hen bird being unable to lay an egg that is ready to come out. Properly fed and housed Australian parakeets rarely will be troubled with egg binding. If affected, the hen bird will look positively sick, sitting hunched up with puffed-out plumage, often on the floor of the aviary (seldom *in* the nest box). With the exception of a heaving of the tail she will sit quite still and usually is easy to catch in the hand. You will be able to feel the stuck egg in the lower part of her abdomen.

Under normal conditions, the egg spends no more than 24 hours in the wide section of the ovary leading to the cloaca, and the cloaca itself. At the right time, muscles in the lower end of the ovary push it into the cloaca and then entirely out of the body. The muscles involved can fail to function properly as a result of stress brought about by chilling, colds, overbreeding, old age, malnutrition (especially deficiency of calcium, phosphorus, and/ or certain vitamins), too young to breed, and so on. Shell-less, or thin shelled eggs (wind eggs) brought about by a deficiency of calcium or some malfunction in the deposit of calcium in the eggshell, also can lead to egg binding though the muscles may be working perfectly well. Because the egg is soft, the muscles are depressing it rather than moving it, so it virtually becomes stuck.

Egg binding usually can be prevented by ensuring that the birds get a balanced diet, including green food and sprouted seed. To prevent wind eggs, ensure that the birds have enough calcium, especially calcium phosphate. Commercial brands of bird grit contain the essential minerals, so ensure that your birds always have some available. Sterilized and crushed and dried chicken eggshells and cuttlebone are also good sources of calcium that always should be available. During the breeding season, a little milk-soaked bread with grated cheese will not go amiss. To further reduce the possibility of egg binding, do not allow your birds to breed too early in the season. The temperature and humidity probably will not be right. In the colder states, do not start breeding until the end of March to mid-April.

Egg binding usually can be cured quite easily if you catch it in time, therefore keep a close eye on your breeding hens. Apply a few drops of warmed (but not too hot!) mineral oil in the cloaca, using a dropper; this will lubricate the passage of the egg. Then put the hen in a hospital cage and maintain the temperature at 90° F (32° C). Warmth will help the bird lay the egg. An avian veterinarian also can treat egg binding by injecting the bird with medicines to stimulate contractions of the oviduct. Sometimes the veterinarian may recommend surgical removal of the egg, by which the egg remains intact. It also can be removed using the aspiration technique, but the egg will be lost in such a case.

Egg Pecking

Not really a disease, egg pecking is a grave nuisance. There really is no cure for a bird that starts egg pecking and it must be removed from the aviary and not used for breeding (perhaps it can be tamed and trained as a pet bird). Chances of egg pecking are very small when the birds are kept in optimum conditions. In case one has valuable breeding birds, it is best to remove the egg(s) immediately. The eggs may be artificially incubated or given to surrogate parents.

Eye Disorders

Birds are subject to several conditions affecting the eyes. In most cases the problem results from complications of colds and resulting secondary infections caused by bacteria or viruses. However, sore eyes can develop from a deficiency in vitamin A or perhaps irritation caused by aerosols or dust. Infected eyes are usually partly closed and have inflamed edges (blepharitis) and a teary discharge.

Bacterial infections of the eye can be brought about by unclean conditions in the aviary, especially dirty perches. Birds frequently wipe their beaks on perches and can soon pick up an infection. Imported birds that have been confined in overcrowded crates often are infected. Check newly imported birds for eye infections (as well as other diseases).

A bird with infected eyes should be placed in a warm environment, preferably a hospital cage. Rinse the eye with a 5 percent boracic solution, or apply an antibiotic ophthalmic ointment two or three times per day (ophthalmic Neosporin or Neopolycin are good commercial products). A few days of treatment usually are sufficient to assure a speedy recovery. (Note: Be conservative when applying ophthalmic ointments. Feathers around the eye and cere ultimately can be lost if they remain covered with the greasy material.)

Cnemidocoptes mites (see scaly face page 67) also can irritate eyelids and eyes when the typical scabs occur in the eye region. Treat the scabs and the edges of the eye with an ophthalmic antibiotic ointment (Eurax Cream). Highly effective against this parasite is the injectable medication Ivermectin (Equalan). Remember to have new binds examined by an avian veterinarian before they come in contact with other birds, and avoid contact with birds that have an unknown history!

59

The Sick Parakeet

A deficiency of vitamin A in the diet can lead to wart-like bumps on the eyelids. Improvement of the diet will help but the bird should be isolated in any case as these warts also can be a symptom of psittacine pox, a highly infectious disease requiring treatment by an avian veterinarian. Serious eye infections can lead to blindness in one or both eyes, the afflicted eye turning a milky white. Birds that become partially or totally blind can be kept alive in a small cage. In the beginning, place the food and water in shallow dishes on the floor of the cage.

Feather Cysts

These occasionally may occur in Australian parakeets and are caused by the growth of a feather

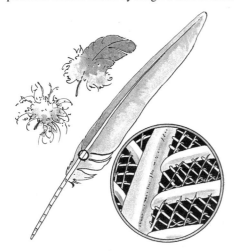

There are three types of feathers: contour feathers (bottom), filoplume feathers (top), and down feathers (left). Contour feathers form the main plumage of the body, wing, and tail, giving the bird its shape and contour. Each contour feather consists of a long stem or rachis, which carries the vane with many barbs (see enlargement). Each barb has interlocking hooks and barbules.
Filoplumes are hairlike feathers with a thin rachis and a fluffy tuft at the tip.
Down feathers provide the insulation for temperature regulation, and have a short rachis and many noninterlocking barbs.

shaft that does not break through the skin. The feather curls up and the more it grows the greater the size of the resulting cyst. If opened up, the cyst will be found to contain a cheese-like substance. A cyst that remains untreated eventually will break open, so that there is a possibility of secondary infection. Occasionally the bird itself pecks the cyst open; on contact with the air, the resultant exudate will harden and form a scab, which continues to grow with the feather and eventually drops off. Birds with several feather cysts should have them and the feathers removed surgically by an avian veterinarian. Any bleeding that occurs can be stopped using styptic wadding or even by fine cauterization. With large wounds, especially those caused by the removal of whole unbroken cysts, it may be necessary to close the wound by suture. Such treatment usually is followed by a course of antibiotics. Cysts on the back or on the tail are best removed wholly; this operation can be performed under local anesthesia, though this is not always necessary.

Feather Plucking

If feather plucking occurs, it usually is associated with the molt and growth of new feathers. It is not difficult to understand that these natural processes cause itching, then scratching, and finally feather plucking. The latter may become a habit and the bird will continue to do it from boredom; at least that is the usual explanation given though there is no actual scientific basis for the fact. Some birds with "nothing else to do" or that are frustrated, become habitual feather pluckers and soon can strip themselves almost naked! Most psittacines can get the habit, but especially cockatoos.

Many wing or tail feathers may be gnawed off at the base leaving just stumps. These must be removed or they are likely to inhibit the growth of replacement feathers. To do this get an assistant to restrain the bird; then hold the wing firmly with one hand and with a pair of forceps, pull out the feather stump at right angles. In case of bleeding, have some styptic wadding on hand. Sometimes a bird

The Sick Parakeet

An Elizabethan colar is used for really persistent feather pluckers. The bird usually gets used to the device within a few days.

can bleed seriously after gnawing at the base of a new feather especially in the wings or tail. You must take immediate action to stop the bleeding or the bird could weaken from loss of blood.

It is interesting to note that most feather plucking parakeets in the United States also are infected with giardiasis, an intestinal protozoan parasite that causes pruritis (severe irritation in the undamaged skin), which can be the cause of the feather plucking. Aviary parakeets in Europe seem to rarely suffer from the disease.

To help discourage feather plucking, the birds first must be given something to keep them occupied. Make sure thay have twigs from fruit trees, willow, or privet; hang several pieces of thick sisal (not synthetic material), string, or rope in the aviary. The birds will spend hours nibbling at these. Examine the diet and decide if its adequate; if not, improve it by providing additional minerals, proteins, and vitamins. Willow twigs contain lignine,

an amino acid that can be effective in stopping feather plucking. Also, make sure that the temperature is not too low and the humidity not too high; that there is good light and ventilation; that the birds have adequate bathing facilities (a weak spray from a hose on warm days is strongly recommended); and ensure that the aviary is not so cluttered with plants, utensils, and other items that the birds don't have freedom of movement.

Persistent feather pluckers must be fitted with an Elizabethan collar, which can be made from stout cardboard and affixed around the neck to prevent them reaching their plumage with their beaks but still allowing them to eat and drink. A bird is likely to lose its desire to pluck its feathers after a few weeks with such a collar, plus improve its diet and accommodations.

Feather plucking can even occasionally lead to cannibalism. All damaged feathers must be removed from a bird; new feathers will replace them in six to eight weeks. If damaged feathers are left on a bird it will gnaw away at them until, sooner or later, it will damage its skin, causing serious bleeding and the possibility of secondary infection. Most Australian parakeets, rosellas, cockatiels, and lovebirds occasionally can develop the habit of plucking their youngsters to baldness. Such plucked young may leave the nest bald on the head, neck, and part of the back. In serious cases the flight and tail feathers may have been plucked out, with possible damage to the feather follicles. Replacement feathers will then grow in a twisted manner.

There are some commercial treatments available for feather plucking. These are usually sprays with a nasty taste, which are claimed to prevent the adults from plucking their young. This seems doubtful when one considers that a bird's sense of taste is poorly developed. Some adults are really persistent in plucking their young. In such cases all one really can do is place the young in the care of reliable foster parents. If no foster parents are available, the young can be placed in a cage in the same aviary as the parents. The mesh in the cage must be wide enough to allow the parents to feed the young through it.

Fractures

Fractures of the leg or wing in captive birds are rare, but usually are caused by depletion of calcium (extensive breeding, nonbreeding hens who constantly are laying eggs, and so on), by rough handling, by the birds being scared and flying into glass or aviary wire, or by being caught by a cat or a dog (however unlikely this may seem—it happens!). Such fractures are best dealt with by an avian veterinarian. However, the more experienced fancier may like to treat the bird himself. Simple fractures in mid-leg or mid-wing can be dealt with as follows: line up the severed sections of wing (or leg) and splint the break on either side with a couple of thin sticks (pieces of bamboo skewer are ideal). Wind bandage around the splints to keep them in place and finally secure with adhesive surgical tape.

As bandages may allow too much movement at the point of fracture (especially with compound fractures or fractures close to the body), an alternative method can be used: the fractured limb is wrapped in small strips of gauze that have been treated with a thin preparatation of plaster of Paris. First wrap the leg twice and hold it in position until the plaster sets; then wrap another couple of strips around the fracture. Compound fractures and other difficult cases are best left to your avian veterinarian.

A torn muscle sometimes can be mistaken for a broken leg. This condition can be caused by a bird frantically trying to free itself after being caught (usually by an overlong nail) in the wire mesh. Torn muscles do not heal easily. You can try to immobilize the affected leg with a bandage, keeping it stable while nature takes its course. A bird with a fracture or torn muscle should be kept in a hospital cage without perches until it is completely healed. Cover the cage bottom with peat moss; keep in subdued light in a quiet location so that the injured bird will move as little as possible. Put food and

water in easy reach and ensure that the bird gets adequate vitamins and minerals.

A broken, drooping wing can be best bandaged with gauze. A slit is cut in the gauze and the folded wing passed through it. It is then wrapped around the body and secured to a leg to keep it from sliding off. Ensure that the bandage is tight but without squeezing the bird uncomfortably. The bird should again be placed in a dark, quiet place for several weeks. Use a cage without perches and with a low roof so the bird will not attempt to fly. In some cases it may be necessary to fit an Elizabethan collar to the treated bird to stop it from pecking at the injury.

French Molt or Psittacine Beak and Feather Disease (PBFD)*

Several Australian parakeets (for example turquoisine, Bourke, and splendid mutations) are subject to French molt or PBFD, though fortunately it is an infrequent occurrence. PBFD is the fear of many bird breeders and it normally starts in young birds while they are still in the nest. The cause of PBFD still is not completely understood, though several theories exist and there is now evidence to suggest that a small DNA-virus could be the culprit. The typical symptoms of PBFD are that birds about to fledge suddenly will shed or break their newly acquired flight and tail feathers. It is usually the primary flight feathers and the tail feathers that are affected, but in serious cases most of the feathers on the body can drop out! It is a pathetic sight to see these naked or half naked birds running about. However, some cases of PBFD are so minor as to be almost completely indetectable; some birds just losing a few tail feathers and still being able to fly. It is interesting to note that in PBFD the feathers are

---

* In Europe and North America, PBFD and French molt are considered to be two distinct diseases, whereas in Australia they are thought to be caused by the same agent (Branson W. Ritchie, DVM, PhD: Proceedings Annual Conference, Association of Avian Veterinarians, 1990, pages 12–24).

often lost symetrically. A daily inspection of the patients will reveal that the first affected feathers are usually the inner primaries and only growing ones are lost; fully grown ones are not affected.

At the present time we still cannot do much about a case of PBFD. You could breed birds for many years without seeing a sign of the disease, and then it suddenly may appear, for no apparent reason. Birds bred on the colony system can produce perfectly healthy youngsters, whereas pairs in the same aviary can produce young that develop PBFD! Those that produce youngsters with PBFD should be stopped from breeding.

Frostbite

Crisp winter days and nights pose the possibility of frostbite, usually in the toes. Birds hanging on to the wire mesh (those that have had a scare in the night from a cat or similar are likely to do this until daylight) are very susceptible. Thin perches also can be a problem as the birds' toes cannot be protected with its feathers. Use thick perches, especially in the sleeping quarters, which should be as draft-proof as possible. There is no cure for frostbite; the frozen part will turn black and eventually drop off. To prevent secondary infection, the resulting wound can be treated with an antiseptic such as noncaustic tincture of iodine applied with a cotton swab.

Goiter

This is an abnormal enlargement of the thyroid, which at one time was quite common in Australian parakeets, cockatiels, budgerigars, and lovebirds. Improvements in diet have led to a decline in the occurrence of the disease, though it still may occur in areas where water is deficient in iodine. Commercial bird sands and grits contain adequate iodine to prevent the disease. One also may purchase specific iodine preparations for the treatment of the condition.

Goiter is easily recognized by the external swelling of the bird's neck. The growth is internal and

may apply pressure to the bird's crop and windpipe causing the bird to become breathless. Breathing heavily, it will drop to the ground, often with wings outspread and with a pendulous crop and neck. It also may emit a high-pitched wheezing sound as its breathes laboredly. To help it breathe more easily, the bird may rest its beak against the bars of the cage or on a parallel branch or perch.

You must take immediate action or the condition will worsen. The bird may start to walk in circles—a symptom of cerebral infection. Asphyxiation, heart failure, or weakness due to insufficient food may then lead to rapid death. Iodine glycerine may be used to treat this disorder; the mixture for Australian parakeets being one part tincture of iodine to five parts glycerine. Alternatively, nine parts paraffin oil to one part iodine glycerine can be administered into the beak with a plastic dropper five times per day over three days and usually will work wonders. If the condition persists, consult your avian veterinarian.

Mites

Several kinds of mites can affect Australian parakeets. Feather mites are divided into the nonpathogenic types, which live on the skin as well as on the feathers, and other, very small mites, which burrow into the shaft and follicle. The first, *Syringophilus bipectioratus*, may be found in wild birds, cockatiels, Australian parakeets, canaries, and pigeons, among others. It feeds on feather and skin debris and although it causes no direct damage, it can cause irritation leading to scratching and feather plucking. The second kind of mite, *Dermoglyphus elongatus*, is more serious, as it burrows into the feather structure.

Good hygiene is the way to keep your birds free of mites as well as other external parasites. Keep the aviary as clean as possible; have permanent facilities for birds to bathe (except outdoors in freezing weather for obvious reasons) and keep wild birds away by whatever means possible. These precautions will also control the red bird-mite (poultry mite) *Dermanyssus gallinae*. This species normally does not live permanently on the bird's body (but may do so in small numbers for a few days at a time) but dwells in cracks and crevices in or around the birds' cage or aviary, coming out at night to feed on the blood of the birds. In severe infestations, millions of these mites (which are difficult to see during the day as they are concealed) can cause untold misery to aviary birds, which quickly will weaken through irritation, stress, and lack of sleep. A single mite does not take a lot of blood but in numbers the pests can take enough to cause severe anemia. They also can transmit blood-bearing diseases from one bird to the next and cause havoc among your breeding birds and their young.

Make daily inspections of your aviaries to look for signs of red bird-mite. A magnifying glass will help, but a better way to diagnose the presence of these pests is to cover a cage with a white cloth or drape one in the corner of the birds' sleeping quarters. Mites will hide in the folds of the cloth and, if present, will appear the next morning as minute red spots. Destroy by burning or soaking in methylated spirits before washing and using again. Remove birds from their cage or aviary and thoroughly spray, clean, and disinfect.

Red mites can live for several months without a blood meal, and at such times are difficult to see as they become translucent when not feeding. Thus birds introduced to an apparently clean aviary that has been unoccupied for a time can be attacked suddenly by mites. At a temperature of 68° F (20° C), the mites can reproduce every five days. Although they stop breeding at low temperatures, adults can survive in outdoor aviaries even in times of severe frost. Wild birds, such as starlings, sparrows, and pigeons, can introduce red mites and other parasites to your aviaries simply by sitting on the roof of the flight and scratching, preening, or ruffling the plumage; otherwise they can be introduced with new stock, especially birds from large stock aviaries.

A good insecticide to use around your birds (one that is effective against the red mite and other parasites) is a compound containing pyrethrins, derived from the pyrethrum flower (a kind of chrysanthemum grown expressly for this purpose, especially in East Africa). Pyrethrins are harmless to vertebrate animals (thus including birds and ourselves) but lethal to ticks, lice, fleas, mites, mosquitos, and other pests. However, if not used properly, pyrethrins can be toxic to birds. It has been shown that pyrethrins can reduce the reproductive capacity of birds. These compounds should, therefore, be used judiciously.

Having removed the birds, apply pyrethrin to all parts of cages, aviaries, utensils, and so on, but remove food first and allow all surfaces to dry out before replacing birds. Special pyrethrin preparations can be obtained to apply directly onto the birds, either from your veterinarian or pet suppliers. Pay special attention to areas around the vent and under the wings. The treatment should be repeated after ten days to eliminate any pests that have hatched from eggs in the intermittent period.

Molt

This is not a disease condition but a natural phenomenon. However, there are many health problems that affect or are affected by molt. The feathers of birds are subject to a great deal of wear and tear. They wear them every day and night—just imagine if we had just one set of clothes and wore them every day and night for a whole year—we certainly would need a new set after that! A bird's feathers are subjected to high temperatures, low temperatures, winds, and frosts, to rain and to bathing, to sand bathing, preening, flying, and so on. Birds therefore change their plumage once per year; in fact Australian parakeets (and other psittacines) molt during the whole year, with the high point just after the breeding season when the young have become independent. This indicates that the functions of the reproductive organs are closely connected with the molt. Additionally, a normal, trouble-free change of plumage is dependent on the season, the temperature, the humidity, and the birds' diet. The molt usually is more intense and complete after a warm spring and good beginning to the summer than it is during cold, wet months. Sometimes a bird will be so eager to molt that it continually will shake its feathers and even pluck some out with its beak gaining some obvious relief when doing so. In most cases however, the molt is also a period of rest and recuperation and the birds will avoid unnecessary activity. During the normal molt, a bird's average body temperature is raised temporarily—during a bad molt, however, the temperature may decrease. As feathers consist of 88 percent protein, it is essential that the birds receive a protein-rich diet prior to and during the molt. At the time of the molt, birds are most susceptible to bone fractures due to the resorption of calcium from the bone tissue. Birds lacking in dietary protein will possibly supplement their diet with their own new feathers! Now and again a bird will lose too many feathers at once and have difficulty in replacing them; this is called an abnormal molt. A bird losing feathers in the wrong season also suffers abnormal molt. Abnormal molts usually are caused by extreme environmental factors such as unusually high or low temperatures, sudden weather changes, shock, disease, or fear. Malfunction of the thyroid gland is a common cause of abnormal molt.

Shock molt is a form of abnormal molt brought on by shock or fear; especially among birds that are new to a particular aviary or cage. Such newly acquired birds always should be treated with utmost care and consideration, and left as quietly as possible to get accustomed to their new surroundings.

Young birds also should be left in peace so that they gradually can get used to their keeper and surroundings. Do not disturb birds at night and keep away such animals as cats, owls, weasels, mice, rats, and so on by any means possible so that they don't cause shock molt in your birds. I have seen birds suffer from shock molt when moved at night for treatment for a totally different disease! With shock molting, the bird usually loses tail and small body feathers but seldom wing feathers. The shedding of tail feathers can be compared with autotomy (or tail shedding) in many lizard species. A predator ends up with a mouthful of tail feathers while its owner makes a quiet escape!

Some Australian parakeets may have a "permanent molt," usually brought about by a deficiency of some amino acids in their diet. In such cases, the normal molt also may be incomplete. A menu adjustment is usually all that is required to solve the problem. Ensure that the birds get adequate plant and animal proteins by following the information given in the Feeding and Food chapter (see page 27). Also provide comfortable housing and protect from extreme weather conditions. During cold weather, supplementary heating (in the form of ceramic lamps, for example) can be provided in the bird's night quarters or indoor cage. Broad spectrum lighting (lighting with some of the qualities of natural daylight/sunlight), such as Vita-Lite, has proven beneficial for birds during the long, gloomy winter days and has had a significant influence on a bird's biological functions. Vita-Lite is also of great benefit to birds that normally are kept indoors and have little access to natural unfiltered sunlight.

Obesity

Some captive birds may get overweight for a number of reasons. Lack of exercise in too small a cage or aviary is a common cause, as is boredom by not having enough things to occupy the bird other than eating. A bad diet, including a choline deficiency, also causes obesity. The process of becoming too fat will take a long time and bird owners must be on the alert for signs of obesity. Once a bird can hardly sit on its perch, things already have gone too far. It may sit on the floor, lethargic and panting. It loses its streamlined shape, becoming heavy and cylindrical. When the feathers of the breast or abdomen are blown aside, the yellow fat deposits can be seen showing through the skin. An obese bird will have its lifespan reduced, will have difficulty in molting, and generally just sits looking thoroughly bored.

You must ensure that your birds do not get overweight, or if they already are overweight, you must take corrective action. First, make sure they have adequate space and facilities for exercise. Caged parakeets and cockatiels must be released in a secure area every day and allowed to fly freely for an hour or so. Hang up a few strong sisal ropes; give a few twigs, and sprays of millet; most parakeets will love to play with these and get plenty of exercise from doing so.

The next anti-obesity action you should take is to ensure that your birds are getting a balanced but not too fattening diet (go strictly by the book if necessary). If birds are too fat, stop giving oily seeds, such as sunflower seeds, but do not starve the bird—however fat it is, it must have a daily food supply! Hence present a good seed mixture and the vitamins choline and methionine, which are involved in fat metabolism and avoid an excess of fat deposition in many of the organs, especially the liver (fatty-liver disease). Excellent sources for these vitamins are yeast and fishmeal.

Preen Gland, Infection of

The preen gland is situated above the base of the tail and secretes oils used in conditioning the plumage. Occasionally this gland may become infected and, if the orifice becomes blocked, an abscess may form. The bird will be pained or irritated and may peck and scratch at the badly swollen area, even plucking out adjacent feathers. The abscess eventually will burst, leaving blood on perches. The conscientious bird keeper, however, does not allow the condition to reach this stage. An infection usually arises from overproduction of the preening secretion, so you can relieve the symptoms somewhat by gently squeezing out the gland at regular intervals. If this does not help, it will be necessary to consult an avian veterinarian, who will incise the abscess and then squeeze out the contents. Further treatment with antibiotics and something to stop the

bleeding may be necessary. Similar symptoms are caused by a tumor of the preen gland. Such a case is more serious than a simple abscess, but the tumor usually is benign and often can be removed successfully by a veterinarian.

Psittacosis (Chlamydiosis)

Sometimes called ornithosis, this disease is transmitted by a number of pet/domestic/farm/feral, and wild bird species, farm stock, and even cats, and can be caught by humans, in which case the victim usually starts with cold symptoms and can progress to a lung infection. At one time the disease was very dangerous, but the advent of antibiotics has removed this danger somewhat, provided you get timely diagnosis and treatment. Modern quarantine regulations in most countries have now also alleviated the banning of imports of some bird species into many countries.

The disease is caused by an obligate, intracellular, heterogenous pathogen—*Chlamydia psittaci*—distinguished from other microorganisms by its unique growth cycle. Unhygienic accommodations, especially during breeding, can trigger outbreaks of psittacosis. The disease also can be brought in by imported birds (especially smuggled birds). Be suspicious of dirty looking birds, especially if they have closed or runny eyes or are blinking excessively. They may look otherwise healthy, but if you accept them you may be asking for trouble.

The disease has a variety of symptoms, which makes it difficult to diagnose in its earlier stages. It usually starts with a heavy cold; a runny nose, wheezing, gasping, lethargy, and often diarrhea. The bird will lose its appetite and there are often symptoms of cramps, lameness, and seizures before the bird dies.

There is a mild form of psittacosis that often can be completely cured but remember that apparently cured birds still can be carriers of the pathogen that can affect other birds and humans too. It is extremely important to report any suspected case of

The Sick Parakeet

the disease in the United States to an avian veterinarian or the Public Health Service.

In general, imported parrots have to be quarantined for 30 days on arrival and are given preventive treatment with 1 percent chlortetracycline or doxycycline premixed with the food or drinking water. These drugs also may be used to treat the disease over 45 days by intramuscular or subcutaneous injection, administered by your avian veterinarian. Sore eyes as a result of the disease can be washed with 0.9 percent saline solution and treated with antimycoticum drops.

Salmonella (Paratyphoid)

There are numerous strains of salmonella bacteria found in many parts of the world. Many of these are harmless but others cause many fatalities in young parakeets and other birds. The rod-like bacteria cause diarrhea, painful joints, and nervous disorders. (In 1967 some *Neophema* species were found to suffer from a nervous disease that caused them to twist their heads around and eventually lose all sense of balance and direction. The salmonella bacterium was first put to blame for this condition, but it has now been verified that the cause is a paramyxovirus type 3 [paramyxovirus type 1 causes New Castle Disease]. To date there is no known cure. Patients should be placed in a hospital cage and given a vitamin B complex supplement. The veterinarian can treat with broad spectrum antibiotics.) Salmonella bacteria are passed in the droppings of infected birds, or via the saliva (when parent birds feed their young). Salmonella also can penetrate the eggshell and infect the unborn embryo.

Four different categories of the disease can occur, often simultaneously. *Intestinal form:* The bacteria attack the intestinal lining, causing diarrhea with foul smelling, soupy, greenish or brownish droppings, often containing undigested food particles (a green color in the droppings also can indicate an infection of the gallbladder—consult a veterinarian immediately). *Joint form:* Intestinal

infections can lead to bacteria invading the bloodstream and infecting all parts of the body including the bone joints. Intense swelling of the joints are accompanied by great pain, which causes the bird to sit still and not move about. *Organ form:* All internal organs can be infected once the bacteria are in the bloodstream, including the liver, kidneys, pancreas, heart, and various other glands. The sick bird is inactive and becomes short of breath and nearsighted. *Nervous form:* If the nerves and spinal column become infected with salmonella, there may be a loss of balance and crippling. Other typical symptoms include awkward turning of the head, fouling of the cloaca, and cramp-like contractions of the toes.

Once infected with salmonella a bird will start getting serious intestinal problems in three to four days. The bacteria multiply in the walls of the intestine, eventually migrating into the bloodstream. Young birds, having no immunity, quickly fall victim to the disease and die, but older, more resistant birds can incubate the disease over long periods and, if not adequately cured, can become lifelong carriers, infecting other birds through their droppings or via their oviducts.

High numbers of casualties in the breeding season often are a sign of salmonellosis in the stock. Have a veterinarian examine dead birds and blood samples. The most used medicines for the treatment of salmonellosis are chloramphenicol, furaldaltone, and trimethoprim-sulpha. After three weeks, the feces should be examined, and again after three months.

From the above, it is apparent that it is very common for an aviculturist to misinterpret an ill bird. In the best interest of the patient, it is recommended to establish a firm relationship with a competent avian veterinarian.

Scaly Face

Scaly face is caused by a burrowing mite *(Cnemidocoptes pilae)*, which quickly can spread from one bird to the next. These little arachnoid parasites burrow into the outer layers of skin where they lay eggs, usually around the eyes and beak but occasionally on the legs and feet. If untreated, the resulting rough, scaly growths gradually will increase and severe deformities of the beak can occur.

Though not a dangerous infection, it is an unpleasant one that merits great care to be sure it is eradicated completely. Fortunately, Australian parakeets in general seem to be less frequently infected with scaly face than budgerigars, in which the disease is quite common. Remove any scaly scabs that fall off as quickly as possible and burn them if you can. The infected birds should be placed in isolation quarters and treated by applying benzyl benzoate, petroleum jelly, or glycerine to the affected area. Mineral oil also can be used but be sure not to get it on the bird's plumage (use a cotton swab). In serious cases, the veternarian may apply Eurax cream or inject with Ivermectin (Equalan). After an infection, thoroughly clean and disinfect the cages and aviaries and all utensils before replacing the birds.

Sour Crop

This arises as a result of a blockage of the crop exit, due to something the bird has eaten—a small feather, for example. Being in the crop for a longer period than usual, the contents will begin to ferment, producing carbon dioxide. As a result the crop becomes swollen with gas and the bird will vomit a frothy fluid, while its head and beak will become stained with mucus. The patient may be held head downwards while you massage the crop gently to expel the gas and some of the accumulated fluid (mainly water). Keep the bird warm and offer it water to which some potassium permanganate has been added. Severe cases may require a minor operation from your avian veterinarian.

Worms

Birds in outdoor aviaries always will be subject to worm infections of one form or another. These internal parasites are brought in by wild birds that let their droppings fall into the aviary.

Roundworms *(Ascaris)*: start as long, white larvae that grow to adulthood in the intestines of the birds that swallow them. The adult worms lay eggs that leave the bird's body in its droppings, ready to infect another bird if taken up. Infested birds quickly lose weight, develop poor plumage, and may suffer from diarrhea or constipation. To confirm a parasite infection, take a stool sample to your avian veterinarian who will be able to diagnose the degree of severity by counting the worm eggs in a sample of feces. The condition can be cured by administering pipera-zine, levamisole, or a similar vermicide as prescribed by the veterinarian. The best prevention is first-rate hygiene and sanitation. Concrete floors can be hosed down regularly to remove infected droppings.

Threadworms *(Capillaria)*: start as round, thread-like parasites that grow to adulthood in a bird's crop or intestine. Again, the eggs of the mature worms leave the body via the droppings. Diarrhea and loss of weight are likely symptoms that can be diagnosed from a stool sample. Piperazine or levamisole can be used as treatment, and good sanitation as prevention. Use Clorox in a 9 percent (or one of the other disinfectants discussed on page 00) solution to clean floors.

Basic Medications and Health Equipment

The conscientious bird keeper will have a stock of basic medications and other first aid items for use in an emergency. This need not be elaborate, but many of the items listed below can be lifesavers (to your birds) in times of need. Expounding on the use of the individual components may be helpful, keeping in mind that most home treatments are palliative prior to the examination and subsequent suggestions of an experienced avian veterinarian.

Gevral Protein, to stimulate appetite. Mix with Mull Soy (in a ratio 1:3), which is also a good source of essential vitamins and minerals. The mixture can be administered with a 2–3 m tube three times per day.

Glucose, as an emergency energy-giving food for sick birds that have not been feeding. The glucose will quickly replace sugars lost from the body.

Kaopectate or Pepto-Bismol, for loose dropping and regurgitation. Soothes and coats the intestines and helps form more solid feces. Two or three drops every four hours administered with a medicine dropper.

Maalox or Digel, for crop disorders. Soothes inflammation and disperses gas. Dosage: two or three drops every four hours.

Karo Syrup, for dehydration and as a provider of energy. Add four drops to 1.5 quarts (1 l) of water. Administer eight to ten drops slowly in the mouth every 20–30 minutes with a medicine dropper.

Monsel solution or styptic powder, to stop bleeding—but don't use the latter close to the beak.

Milk of Magnesia, for constipation. Do not use it, however, if the bird has heart or kidney problems. Dosage: three to five drops in the mouth with a dropper, twice daily for two days.

Mineral oil, for constipation, crop impaction, or egg binding. Use two drops in the mouth for two days administered by a dropper. When administering mineral oil, take care that it doesn't enter the respiratory tract as it can cause pneumonia, vitamin deficiencies, and possibly other problems.

Hydrogen peroxide, 3 percent activated charcoal (of Milk of Magnesia), for poisoning. Use to induce vomiting, to absorb the substance, and to speed its passage through the digestive tract. Ask your avian veterinarian for more details.

Goodwinol, mineral oil, Scalex, Eurax, Vaseline, for scaly face and/or scaly leg.

Betadine, Domeboro solution, A&D ointment, Neosporin, Neopolycin, Mycitracin, Aquasol A, for skin irritations. Domeboro is used on a wet dressing; dissolve 1 teaspoon or tablet in a pint of water. A&D is excellent for small areas. Neosporin, Neopolycin, and Mycitracin contain antibiotics. Aquasol A is a cream and contains vitamin A. All these ointments and creams can be applied to the infected area twice daily.

Lugol's iodine solution, for thyroid enlargement (goiter). Half a teaspoon of Lugol with 1 ounce of water; place one drop of this mixture in one ounce of drinking water daily for two to three weeks.

Further health equipment would include:

Heat source, Infrared lamp (60–100 watt bulb).

Hospital cage, several commercial models are available or you can make your own.

Environmental thermometer, buy one that is easy to read.

Cage covering, use a cage covering if you do not have a hospital cage. Towels or baby blankets are fine.

Adhesive or masking tape, use a half-inch roll.

Sterile gauze pads.

Cotton-tipped swabs.

Needle-nosed pliers and/or tweezers.

Sharp scissors with rounded ends (baby nail scissors).

Feeding tubes, use 8F or 10F tubes, which many veterinarians carry. Ask your veterinarian to demonstrate the technique of tube feeding.

Syringes or plastic medicine droppers, for administering oral medication.

Heredity and Mutations

During the last fifteen years or so, the breeding of color mutations in Australian parakeets has attracted a great deal of attention. Not everyone is charmed by the results, however, and many fanciers remain faithful to the original, wild-colored birds. Nevertheless, it would be a shortcoming not to cover this exciting new branch of the hobby, especially because interest in mutations is increasing rapidly.

Although it will not be possible to delve deeply into the subject of genetics, I will try to explain the essential principles as simply and practically as possible. Note well, however, that some time and patience will be required of anyone who has not previously studied the subject.

Colors

The three factors that produce all of the color variants seen in psittacines include changes in the (1) pigment melanin, (2) pigment carotenoid, and (3) structure color blue.

Melanin: the dark pigment of the feathers, eyes, beak, feet, and nails—in other words, the colors black, gray, and brown. The color of human hair mainly is due to melanin.

Carotenoid: the bright pigments, which can occur in feathers and beak—specifically the colors yellow, orange, and red.

Structure Color: blue (and violet). The term *structure color* indicates that the color is related to the *structure* of the feather. In other words, blue plumage is not the result of a distinctive pigment; rather, it is a physical effect produced by the structural arrangement of molecules on the feather's surface.

You will have noticed that the color green has not been mentioned. This is because green, which is not a primary color, results from a combination of the carotenoid pigment color yellow and the structure color blue. If the yellow fails in a green bird, the result is a blue bird; if the blue fails, the result is a yellow one.

Mutations

Mutations in the psittacine species generally are caused by changes in the melanin and the carotenoid, and only occasionally in the structure color. We therefore can concern ourselves mainly with the changes in melanin and carotenoid. The following are the most usual forms.

Pastel: In this mutation, the *quantity* of melanin is reduced. The colors of the wild form are retained in lighter, diluted form—frequently as light, grass-green. The yellow turquoisine parakeet is an example of this mutation.

Lutino, albino, yellow: In these mutations, melanin is completely or almost completely lacking. In lutinos and albinos, melanin is absent from all parts of the body—feathers, eyes, beak, feet, and nails. In yellow, melanin is absent only from the plumage. Lutinos and albinos are therefore easily recognizable by their red eyes; normal yellows have dark eyes. Lutinos and albinos differ from each other in that the former still has its carotenoid and, therefore, will show some yellow, orange, and/or red, whereas the latter has lost these colors as well as the melanin colors, leaving a pure white bird with red eyes. For that matter, when melanin is totally absent, the structure color (blue) becomes white.

Pied, opaline: Here, the melanin is absent from parts of the plumage. The pied mutation usually has a patchy, irregular color pattern, with white or yellow patches where the melanin is absent. There is a great variety of pied patterns, ranging from a few affected feathers to large areas of the plumage.

This mutation must not be confused with the results of an inadequate diet. A deficiency of the amino acid lysine in the diet, for example, can result in an inadequate formation of melanin. Thus, some green feathers can become yellow, whereas black ones can become very pale gray to whitish. An improvement in the diet will result in normalization of the plumage after the following molt.

The second mutation in this category is the opaline. Here, the carotenoid becomes more in-

Heredity and Mutations

tense. Light yellow becomes deep yellow, medium yellow becomes near orange, and pink becomes near red. The opaline mutation is difficult to recognize, as its outward appearance varies from species to species.

In the red rosella, virtually the whole underside and tail are red; red also can be seen in the back markings.

The rose Bourke is also a brilliant example of the opaline mutation. The normal yellowish color is replaced by a pure pink, and the melanin is lost in the mantel, back, secondary flight feathers, and head. This arrangement is similar to that of the budgerigar (parakeet), in which the mantel has no markings; in the Bourke this also applies to part of the wings.

The pearled (or opaline) cockatiel shows a totally different variation. Melanin is absent from the center of the feather, so that each affected feather is white or yellow with a dark edge. This gives a checkered effect, seen most often on the wings. The yellow of the pearled is lighter than that of a normal gray cockatiel.

Young cockatiel males are like normal gray cocks. The back of the neck, mantle, and wings are covered with white or yellow pearly markings. After approximately 6–12 months, the males molt into their adult plumage, being normal gray (wild form). The hens, however, keep their beautiful pearling. Eyes, beak, feet, and legs are as in normal gray.

Cinnamon, fallow: In these mutations, the color of the melanin is changed: black is replaced by brown. In cinnamons, brown predominates; fallows show a brown-gray that is particularly obvious on the primary wing feathers.

These mutations give varying outward appearances, depending on the bird species. The effects are more obvious in a cockatiel than in a Bourke or a Kakariki. Green becomes lighter in color and more yellowish; gray becomes more brown-gray.

An interesting difference between the cinnamon and the fallow is that although the young of both are hatched with red eyes, the cinnamon gets dark eyes within a week and the fallow retains the red eyes. There can, therefore, be no confusion with yellow mutations, which are hatched with dark eyes.

Seagreen: In this mutation, the carotenoid is diminished. The plumage, therefore, shows less yellow, orange, and/or red. In a good sea green mutation, the carotenoid is reduced by half. There are variations. Less carotenoid produces a more bluish bird; more carotenoid gives a greener one. An example is the sea green splendid parakeet.

Blue: A pure blue bird has melanin and, of course, the structure color blue. Because carotenoid is absent, yellow, orange, and red tints are totally missing.

The white face or charcoal cockatiel also is included in this group. Here, too, the yellow and red are missing, but because the wild color is not green the mutation produces white rather than a blue plumage.

Principles of Heredity

We will now consider the means by which the mutations are inherited. This, in turn, determines what the offspring of various combinations will look like.

Dominant: If one of the parent birds is purebred (see below) for the dominant color, all of the young will take on that color. In other words, the purebred dominant suppresses all other colors, even though the offspring carry other colors in their genetic material (or *genes*). Colors hidden in the genes can emerge later in particular pairings. In general, the wild color is dominant. (If two birds are purebred for the dominant color, all of the offspring also will be purebred for the dominant color.)

Recessive: If two recessive-colored birds are bred, the offspring also will be of the recessive color. However, if a dominant bird is paired with a recessive bird, all the young will take on the color of the dominant bird. The recessive color is thus hidden.

Heredity and Mutations

TABLE I Yellow x the Normal Form (= Wild Color)

	PARENTS			YOUNG	
Male		**Female**		**Males**	**Females**
1. Normal	x	Yellow	=	50% Normal/Yellow	50% Normal/Yellow
2. Yellow	x	Normal	=	50% Normal/Yellow	50% Normal/Yellow
3. Normal/Yellow	x	Normal	=	25% Normal/Yellow 25% Normal	25% Normal/Yellow 25% Normal
4. Normal	x	Normal/Yellow	=	25% Normal/Yellow 25% Normal	25% Normal/Yellow 25% Normal
5. Normal/Yellow	x	Yellow	=	25% Normal/Yellow 25% Yellow	25% Normal/Yellow 25% Yellow
6. Yellow	x	Normal/Yellow	=	25% Normal/Yellow 25% Yellow	25% Normal/Yellow 25% Yellow
7. Normal/Yellow	x	Normal/Yellow	=	25% Normal/Yellow 12½% Normal 12½% Yellow	25% Normal/Yellow 12½% Normal 12½% Yellow
8. Yellow	x	Yellow	=	50% Yellow	50% Yellow

Purebred (homozygous): A purebred bird possesses only the genes for the revealed color. All recessive-colored birds *must* be purebred. Dominant-colored birds, however, may carry a masked gene of a recessive color.

Split (heterozygous): This means a bird of the dominant color has a hidden color mutation, which can be passed on to its offspring. For example, a green bird with a hidden blue mutation in its genetic makeup is called "split for blue" or "green/blue."

Sex-linked: This means that the inheritance of a particular factor is dependent on sex. For example, hemophilia in humans is carried by females, but is revealed only in males. It is thus important to know which parent has the appropriate colors that, with the sex, will be passed on to the young.

Sex-linked recessive: This means that the recessive gene for a particular factor is associated with the group of genes (or *chromosome*) that determines the sex of the offspring. Remember:

• In dominant heredity there are no split males or females.

• A sex-linked female can never be split for the color.

• In recessive birds, regardless of their gender, both male and female can be split.

Autosomal: This refers to inheritance that is not sex-linked.

Autosomal recessive: means that the gene for the factor in question is not carried on a sex chromosome.

In most cases, the same mutations are inherited by the same means, although there are occasional exceptions to the rules. One example is the lutinos; most inherit sex-linked recessive, but there are also some lutino forms that inherit autosomal recessive (the lutino Princess of Wales parakeet and the lutino Elegant parakeet, for example).

Top: A pair of twenty-eight parakeets. Note the two ▶ most distinguishing features of this species: the narrow red band on the forehead and the greenish underside. Below left: The habitat of the common red-rumped parakeet is open, lightly wooded areas, but it also likes parks and gardens. Below right: A pair of many-colored or mulga parakeets. Known for their quiet and friendly nature, they are rather popular in aviculture.

Heredity and Mutations

Formulas

Most color mutations in Australian parakeets may be dealt with either in the autosomal recessive or in the sex-linked recessive form.

Autosomal recessive inheritance: The subjoining mutations follow the same "rules" of inheritance. You only have to replace the yellow mutation from Table I for one of the listed color mutations.

Simply by replacing "yellow" in Table I for the following mutations, the results are at your fingertips:

Barnard's parakeet	— blue
Bourke's parakeet	— fallow yellow
Cockatiel	— pied silver white face

Elegant parakeet	— lutino
King's parrot	— yellow
Pennant's parakeet	— blue yellow white
Princess of Wales parakeet	— blue lutino albino
Rosella	— pastel
Turquoisine parakeet	— yellow
Splendid parakeet	— sea green pastel blue white-breasted blue

Sex-linked recessive inheritance: The easiest way to explain this inheritance is to study Table II, which deals with wild- or normal-colored and cinnamon colored parent birds:

TABLE II   Cinnamon Splendid Parakeet x the Normal Form (= Wild Color)

PARENTS			YOUNG	
Male		**Female**	**Males**	**Females**
1. Normal	x	Cinnamon	= 50% Normal/Cinnamon	50% Normal
2. Cinnamon	x	Normal	= 50% Normal/Cinnamon	50% Cinnamon
3. Normal/Cinnamon	x	Normal	= 25% Normal/Cinnamon 25% Normal	25% Normal 25% Cinnamon
4. Normal/Cinnamon	x	Cinnamon	= 25% Normal/Cinnamon 25% Cinnamon	25% Normal 25% Cinnamon
5. Cinnamon	x	Cinnamon	= 50% Cinnamon	50% Cinnamon

◀ Top: The rather rare hooded parakeet lives in the wild in tropical, lightly wooded country where the hens nest in termite mounds. Below: A group of good-looking, healthy, young hooded parakeets.

Heredity and Mutations

The mutations below follow the same "rules." Replace "cinnamon" with one of the given colors, and you have the answer:

Bourke's parakeet — rose (pink)
cinnamon
Cockatiel — pearled (laced or opaline)
cinnamon (fawn or isabelle)
lutino
albino
Red-rumped parakeet — yellow (cinnamon)
Red-fronted parakeet — cinnamon
Splendid parakeet — cinnamon

So far, we have dealt only with pairings of one color with the wild (or normal) color. The crossing of mutations is a little more complicated, but even here there are a few simple formulas. To do this, we must bring the autosomal recessive and the sex-linked recessive forms together. There are four possibilities, as shown in Table III.

Table IV provides an example for each of these possibilities. In case you wish to know the end results of certain crossings, you just have to know the heredity status of each parent. The next step is to check in which of the four categories each parent fits. Next, simply replace the given color in the table for the colors you like to put together.

These crossings result in birds that are split for two colors: the first crossing lutino x pearl gives us normal (= wild or gray colored) males that are split for both lutino and pearl. If we replace the lutino male cockatiel in Table IV with a cinnamon male, the end result will be: 50% normal males, split for cinnamon and pearl, and 50% cinnamon hens, and so on.

Some final remarks regarding the albino mutation. The best step to take is pairing a sex-linked lutino male with a recessive blue hen, or the other way around. (See Table V.)

By further combining the right young from Table VI, it is possible to "create" albino offspring:

Additional Considerations

There are two important points that apply to everything discussed in this chapter. The first is that all of the percentages given for results are averages: Do not expect to find the young to be 50 percent cocks and 50 percent hens in every nest. The second

TABLE III Autosomal Recessive x Sex-Linked Recessive

Male	Female
sex-linked recessive	x sex-linked recessive
sex-linked recessive	x autosomal recessive
autosomal recessive	x sex-linked recessive
autosomal recessive	x autosomal recessive

TABLE IV Autosomal Recessive x Sex-Linked Recessive: Examples

PARENTS		YOUNG	
Male	Female	Males	Females
Sex-linked x Lutino Cockatiel	**Sex-linked** Pearl Cockatiel	50% Normal/Lutino/Pearl	50% Lutino
Sex-linked x Lutino Cockatiel	**Recessive** Pied Cockatiel	50% Normal/Lutino/Pied	50% Lutino/Pied
Recessive x Pied Cockatiel	**Sex-linked** Pearl Cockatiel	50% Normal/Pied/Pearl	50% Normal/Pied
Recessive x Yellow Pennant	**Recessive** Blue Pennant	50% Normal/Yellow/Blue	50% Normal/Yellow/Blue

Heredity and Mutations

TABLE V   Albino Mutation: 1

PARENTS		YOUNG	
Male	Female	Males	Females
Lutino	x Blue	50% Normal/Lutino/Blue	50% Lutino/Blue
Blue	x Lutino	50% Normal/Lutino/Blue	50% Normal/Blue

TABLE VI   Albino Mutation: 2

PARENTS		YOUNG	
Male	Female	Males	Females
Normal/Lutino/Blue	x Blue	12½% Normal/Blue 12½% Normal/Lutino/Blue 12½% Blue 12½% Blue/Albino	12½% Normal/Blue 12½% Lutino/Blue 12½% Blue 12½% *Albino*
Normal/Lutino/Blue	x Lutino/Blue	6¼% Normal/Lutino 12½% Normal/Lutino/Blue 6¼% Lutino 12½% Lutino/Blue 6¼% Blue/Albino 6¼% *Albino*	6¼% Normal 12½% Lutino/Blue 6¼% Lutino 12½% Lutino/Blue 6¼% Blue 6¼% *Albino*
Normal/Lutino/Blue	x Normal/Blue	12½% Normal/Blue 12½% Normal/Lutino/Blue 6¼% Normal 6¼% Normal/Lutino 6¼% Blue 6¼% Blue/Lutino	12½% Normal/Blue 12½% Lutino/Blue 6¼% Normal 6¼% Lutino 6¼% Blue 6¼% *Albino*

point is that the results of these formulas will be correct only if you know precisely the genetic makeup of the parents and how the colors are passed on. If different results should arise from those given in the formulas, then you have an unknown hidden color factor in one (or both) of the parents.

There are also certain color forms that are not connected with inheritance. Frequently this happens when birds with slight differences are bred selectively over a long period of time. Consider, for example, the red-bellied turquoisine parakeet and the red-bellied splendid parakeet. These are produced by breeding birds that have a lot of red in their plumage. It is thus worth selecting birds with desirable colors for breeding.

Understanding Australian Parakeets

Introduction

The majority of psittacines described in this book belong to a group known to ornithologists as "broad-tailed parakeets." This name is applied to these charming, ornamental birds because the tail feathers are arranged stepwise; in other words they increase in length from the outside to the center, making the tail look very broad when the feathers are spread. The tail is always longer than the wings and the four central feathers are of equal length.

Broad-tailed parakeets originally would have all been forest dwellers as some of the contemporary species still are (for example members of the genera *Purpureicephalus* and *Lathamus*).

During the gradual drying out of the Australian continent, forests and woodlands decreased in area, being replaced by savannah and the so-called open woodland. Such biotopes are the main habitats of most broad-tailed parakeet species today. But there are some species, Bourke's parakeet for example, that over the (many) years have adapted to even drier regions. In these semidesert areas, night parrots *(Geopsittacus occidentalis)*, Princess of Wales parakeets *(Polytelis alexandrae)* and even budgerigars *(Melopsittacus undulatus)* find themselves at home.

It is understandable that wild birds only breed when adequate food is available. As plant growth is dependent on rainfall and rainfall is scarce in a great part of Australia, annual breeding is not always possible. Most species breed just once per season, but of course the weather patterns must be suitable. In central Australia there may be two, sometimes three, clutches per season, but this, of course, is only possible under optimum weather conditions.

Looking at the southern regions of Australia, we see that the influence of a pleasant spring coupled with an adequate food supply means that many bird species go to nest in August. Thanks to the mainly light but sometimes heavy rainfall of the preceding winter, there is a riot of flowers and seeds, which in turn attract myriads of insects that also are appreci-ated by many parakeets. The "table is set" for many bird species until well into August, through an abundance of half-ripe seeds. Towards the end of November and mid-December, the temperature rises sharply and may remain in excess of 86° F (30° C) for long periods. The rains are over and grasses, shrubs and other food sources dry up, making a shortage of food. This means the end of the breeding season. Sometimes a second wave of light rains in April and May can trigger a second nesting response.

In northern and central Australia, temperatures are suitable all year for successful breeding. The main rains fall from December through April (sometimes later) making these the ideal times for breeding (suitable temperature and moisture). Species such as the golden-shouldered parakeet, paradise parrot, Brown's parakeet, and pale-headed rosella will then start nesting with great enthusiasm. They will continue to breed until the end of the rainy season means a decline in available food.

Professor Dr. Karl Immelmann, who carried out much ornithological fieldwork in the sixties, especially in relation to parakeets and finches, states in his book *Die Australischen Plattschweifsittiche* (Ziemsen, Wittenberg Lutherstadt, 1962) that in central Australia there is no regular rainy season, but the northern summer monsoon rains and the winter westerley rains of the south may occasionally reach inland. Sometimes, deep pressure systems from both regions can move towards the center. Such factors would appear to suggest that rain may occur in any month of the year, but many years can pass with no rainfall whatsoever. The smaller bird species have adapted themselves to this unreliable situation. They have no regular or particular nesting period, but will breed at any time of the year when there is sufficient moisture to trigger an abundance of food items. As the rain is not only unreliable regarding the time of the year, but also to the area in which it falls, birds often breed closely to each other in small areas, sometimes during totally different periods. Under the broad-tailed parakeets, there are mainly five species which have this irregular breeding period *(Melopsittacus undulatus, Nymphicus hollandicus, Polytelis alexandrae, Neopsephotus bourkii,* and *Geopsittacus occidentalis).*

Sedentary or Nomadic?

From the above it is fairly easy to draw a conclusion: in regions where rain falls, birds will go quickly to nest, whereas where temperatures are high and there is no rain, parakeets will not breed. Many birds move from unsuitable to suitable areas. Only in areas where there is always regular rainfall, and thus adequate food, are the birds sedentary in their habits; these areas are primarily coastal.

Groups of birds that dwell in the Australian outback are thus forced to be nomadic in order to find adequate food and water. Once they have found both in adequate supply, they can spend some time

Neophema chrysogaster. The orange-bellied parakeet lives in pairs or small family groups, and is considered rather rare. This shy bird is protected by law.

in such a "fertile" terrain, as long as the situation remains such.

In the real sense there are no genuine "migratory birds" under the broad-tailed parakeets, although some species like the blue-winged parakeet *(Neophema chrysotoma),* the orange-bellied parakeet *(Neophema chrysogaster),* and the swift parakeet *(Lathamus discolor)* are "on the go" annually as they leave Tasmania and fly over the Bass Strait to the mainland in order to avoid the lower winter temperatures of their breeding areas.

Bird lovers who have the possibility of observing Australian broad-tailed parakeets in their native habitats soon will discover that most species are outstanding fliers with great endurance. The "migrators" mentioned above are recognized by their swift, straight flight, with sharp turns; the same can be said for the cockatiels and members of the genus *Polytelis.* All of these species frequently fly at great altitudes. Rosellas, grass parakeets, Bourke's parakeets, and members of the genera *Barnardius, Purpureicephalus,* and *Psephotus* all have a rolling finch-like flight. These species usually fly close over the ground and vegetation. I must point out here that the *Neophoma* species are not quite such enthusiastic fliers and prefer to forage on the ground. When they take off they never fly in a straight line and their flight can be described as similar to the weak fluttering of a butterfly. Should they be traveling over greater distances however, they fly in a straight line high in the air.

The ground parrot, a particularly inept flyer, is a champion clamberer and an amazingly fast runner. All *Neophema* members are also good climbers.

Feeding

The staple diet of all broad-tailed parakeets is ripe seeds, but they also will take many kinds of insects and spiders, especially during the breeding season. These are mainly insects and their larvae found on blossoms and leaves, but also some from the bark, which are pounced upon and devoured with obvious delight! As a change they also will take many kinds of fruits, especially apples and pears, as well as berries, blossom nectar, and eucalyptus blossoms. Stomach examinations have shown that most species also swallow coarse sand, which helps in the grinding up of food in the gizzard.

Many species of parakeet forage on the ground for food, but also in the trees, especially after insects, fruits, nectar, and eucalyptus seeds. It is interesting to note that, like cockatoos, members of the genus *Platycercus* lift food to the beak with the foot (see below). Other kinds will hold a loose twig with seeds, grains, and so on against the ground with the foot, to enable them to extract the tasty parts more easily. In captivity, I have seen most of the broad-tailed parakeets sooner or later pick up food with one of the feet (including *all* of the *Platycercus* species).

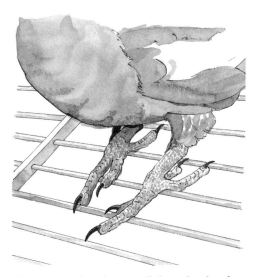

Parrots and parakeets have so-called zygodactylous feet: two toes projecting forward and two projecting backward. They are very susceptible to frostbite.

Before further discussing the use of the feet to assist in feeding, I would like to mention something about "scratching." Most broad-tailed parakeets pass the foot *behind* the wing to scratch the head; this is contrary to the cockatoos, lories, lorikeets, most Africans (lovebirds, for example) and many South American psittacines, which pass the foot *before* the wing to scratch the head. Exceptions are the king parrot *(Alisterus scapularis)* and members of the genus *Polyteris*, which scratch their head in a similar manner to cockatoos. Dr. Immelmann believes that the "behind scratching" is a trait originating from the reptilian ancestry of birds, though birds in the nest scratch themselves "before" a long time; later turning to "behind."

In view of the above, one can imagine that scratching and the picking up of food in the feet are related phenomena; but this is not so! *Platycercus* and *Barnardius* species, for example, can take food in the foot and raise it directly to the beak if necessary, but to scratch the head, the foot goes behind the wing. Lories and lorikeets however do not have the habit of taking food in the foot, but scratch the head before the wing. On this subject, Dr. Immelmann remarks that it is indeed an amusing sight when, for example, a rosella, bringing a piece of food to its beak in the foot, suddenly passes the same foot behind its wing in order to scratch its head—sometimes quite close to the beak itself. Although the foot comes close to the beak in both cases, it passes directly in one case and behind the wing for the other. It is true that the *Platycercus* and *Barnardius* species scratch their heads directly, but should they require a more thorough scratch, the foot always is brought behind the wing in order to reach the head. Dr. Immelmann thinks that perhaps in these two genera, we are seeing the evolutionary transition from one method to another. In the remaining genera of broad-tailed parakeets, neither Dr. Immelmann nor I could observe any similar transition.

I would like to discuss a few generalized points about the drinking habits of broad-tailed parakeets.

Understanding Australian Parakeets

In the wild, I have seen almost all *Platycercus* species, but also cockatiels and golden-shouldered parakeets, go to drink between 1 and 3 P.M. In contrast, the barraband, Bourke's, Brown's (or northern rosella), and turquoisine parakeets slake their thirst in the morning and in the evening. Also, all broad-tailed parakeets like to bathe with the exception of Bourke's. Not only do the birds enjoy a light shower of rain (when they gather high in the trees), but I have seen them take an early morning bath at their drinking venues, whereby they dip the head in the water, plunge, and make shaking motions, so that they dampen themselves down with the wings. The birds never allow the wings to become too waterlogged in case they have to make a quick getaway in time of danger.

Reproduction

During the European settlement of inland Australia since the late eighteenth century, farmers have made storm water dams as drinking holes for their cattle, and artificially irrigated their land by bore or pipeline for the cultivation of crops. Such actions have resulted in dramatic changes to much of the inland environment, some of which have, by no means, been detrimental to many bird species. The extra availability of water and the presence of edible crops means that many parakeet species can now live in areas that previously were barren to them. Birds that follow human habitation and agriculture are known as "culture followers." Unfortunately most of these birds are classified as pests by the fruit growers and farmers, as they can cause enormous damage to orchards and grain crops. It is thus open season all year-round for some bird species which are shot in great numbers. Fortunately, most parakeets are very prolific and manage to keep their numbers at a reasonable level. More serious is the use of poisons in water, on land, and on fruit trees. This poison unfortunately is not selective and kills not only the pest birds but other birds as well as various animals, and can be a great danger to the continuing existence of some species.

One interesting culture follower is the Bourke's parakeet, which during the heat of the day may seek shelter under the veranda of a house!

The development of fruit orchards and grain fields has not been only a benefit to birds. European settlement also has brought dangers to the birds and other forms of native wildlife. The introduction of rabbits *(Orytolagus cuniculus)*, European starlings *(Sturnus vulgaris)*, and European foxes *(Vulpes vulpes)* is an example of some of the difficulties. In eastern Australia, starlings have taken over many of the nest hollows formerly used by parakeets and driven many of them from their original haunts! The ground parrot *(Pezoporus wallicus)* and the night parrot *(Geopsittacus occidentalis)* are, as you know, mainly ground breeders and their eggs and young form all too easy prey for foxes and feral domestic cats. Fortunately, there are in Australia a number of wildlife reserves that are kept free of foxes and cats so that birds can breed undisturbed. In this connection, we can mention the birds of prey as natural enemies of parakeets. The parakeets are searching the skies for signs of danger and forget to look around them, making themselves easy prey to a cat or a fox.

As we already know, broad-tailed parakeets are exclusively hole breeders. They use hollow tree trunks or thick hollow branches. I have found many nests with eggs or young in fallen trees. As you will imagine, such nests cannot be regarded as safe from foxes and cats.

Most parrots and parakeets do not use any nesting materials, and the eggs are deposited directly on the lining of the hollow. Some *Psephotus* species make their nest hollow in termite mounds or in the vertical loam banks of watercourses. The ground parakeet however, is an exclusive ground nester, just like the night parrot, which inhabits the barren, rocky semidesert of central Australia; the former makes an insignificant little platform in the sand with a few grass stems, or will even make do with a bare hollow in the sand; the latter constructs an exquisite nest with spinifex grass. Together with the quaker parakeet of South America and the African lovebirds *(Agapornidae)*, this is one of the few (and in Australia the only) hookbills to construct a substantial nest, in this case in the middle of a spinifex bush, and access to the nest via a narrow tunnel. The bottom of the nest is covered with a thin layer of little twigs so that the brooding hen does not injure herself on the sharp needles of the spinifex. In this connection, it is interesting to note that the painted fire-tailed finch *(Emblema picta)* builds its nest in a similar situation and uses the same precautionary measures.

In normal circumstances, all broad-tailed parakeets lay their four to six eggs between 12 A.M. and 2 P.M., at intervals of around 48 hours, sometimes only 24 hours. As they are hole nesters, the eggs are white in color, requiring no camouflage. The eggs may be matt or glossy. Older hens often lay larger clutches. Brown, swift, splendid, and paradise parakeets are known for their small clutches.

In the wild, the hens begin to incubate after the laying of the next-to-last or last egg. The cock stays close by and stands guard; the barraband and the rock pebbler are exceptions to this as the cocks may be found far from the nest, only going there to feed the hen. With other species also, the cocks go to the nest to feed the hens at particular times. The turquoisine cock feeds only in the mornings and in the evenings. The hen leaves the nest to meet the cock on the ground or on a twig near to the nest. This method of feeding outside the nest is common to all *Neophema* species.

The incubation time for most broad-tailed parakeet species averages 20–21 days; for *Neophema* species and the Bourke's 18–19 days. As incubation may be commenced before the clutch is complete, the young may not all hatch at the same time.

They are fed first by the hen, the cock beginning to help when the young are ten to fourteen days old.

Dr. Immelmann noted that unlike all other parrots, broad-tailed parakeets do not remove droppings from the nest. However, certain grubs feed on the droppings of the young, keeping the nest hollow remarkably clean.

At four to five weeks of age, depending on the size of the species, the young leave the nest. A week after fledging, they already can feed themselves, although the parents will continue to give them tidbits for two or three weeks. At three months of age, they begin the first molt. Smaller species are in full adult plumage after this molt, but the larger kinds have a sort of temporary plumage before coming into full color in their second year.

Social Life

After the breeding season has finished and the dry period has begun, the broad-tailed parakeets form into large groups that go through thick and thin together; these groups can hold enormous numbers of birds, especially in regions where watering facilities are few and far between. When breeding begins again, the pairs depart from the group to seek nesting places and rear a family, without any particular contact with the main group. A clear exception are the *Barnardius* species, which remain paired throughout the year and rarely form groups of more than four to six birds. During the breeding season, a social contact is maintained in the turquoisine-, rock-pebbler, swift, red-rumped, and Princess of Wales parakeets.

Cocks and hens show their affection to each other by mutual preening, feeding each other and so on especially among the *Neophema* species. In the *Platycercus* species however, mutual preening is not carried out.

The Species

Turquoise Grass Parakeet— *Neophema pulchella*

Neophema: new sound; *pulchella:* beautiful, fine, pretty.

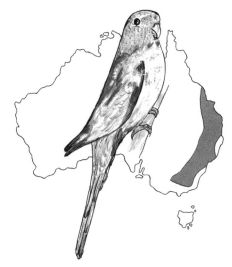

Neophema pulchella. The turquoise (or turquoisine) grass parakeet is a friendly species that can be housed in an aviary with finches, doves, and various Australian parakeets that don't belong to the genus *Neophema.*

Description: The cock has a blue face; the underside is yellow with green highlights, becoming paler near the tail; sometimes there is a reddish tinge on the lower belly. The neck, throat, most of the wings, and the back are green. There is a blue patch in the wing (shoulder) and also a blue stripe along the wing; the primaries are also blue. The tail coverts are green; the outer tail feathers are yellow; the underside of the tail is also yellow. The eyes are dark brown, the beak is black, and the feet are blackish-brown. The hen lacks the red shoulder patch and has less blue on the head; the eyes are surrounded by yellow; the breast is more green. The lower underside is pale yellow, as is beneath the tail.

Young males develop the red shoulder patches early in life and are in full color in eight to ten months. These birds may be used for breeding at twelve months of age.

Size: 8 inches (20 cm) including the 4-inch (10-cm) long tail. Weight: cock, 1⅓ to 1⅔ ounces (36–45 g); hen, 1⅓ ounces (38 g). Leg band: ¹¹⁄₆₄ inch (4 mm).

Voice: A soft but quite penetrating, double-noted whistle, similar to that of the blue-winged grass parakeet.

Nest: In a hollow branch or trunk; the entrance being usually not more than 3.5 feet (1 m) above the ground. The hen lays four to seven roundish ⅞ by ²³⁄₃₂ inch (22 x 18 mm) white eggs on a layer of rotted wood chips. The hen incubates on her own for about 18 days, but the cock feeds her mainly early mornings and evenings. He feeds her from outside the nest entrance. He hardly feeds the young until they are approximately fourteen days old. The young leave the nest at about four weeks of age.

Distribution: Found in Central Queensland, south through New South Wales (this species has bred close to Sydney) to the border with Victoria. They live mainly in open woodland, close to water, grassland, or mountain slopes. The species is far from abundant in the wild; though it is not uncommon in aviaries.

Remarks: Turquoises live in pairs or small groups, foraging close to the ground in search of seeds. They are partly crepuscular, and appear to drink just once per day, often before the first light. The species was discovered in 1788 and first thoroughly described by Shaw in 1792.

Breeding pairs should be provided with a nest box 15¾ inches (40 cm) deep and 8 inches (20 cm) square, with a layer of damp wood chips and mulch in the base. The entrance hole should be about 2⅓ inches (6 cm) in diameter.

During the breeding season, unlike all *Neophema* species, these birds must have a supply of low-fat milk- or water-soaked stale white bread, germinated seed, the normal seed menu (millet, panicum, canary grass seed, small sunflower seed), a rich variety of green food and fresh twigs with buds. Only birds bred in captivity should be allowed to overwinter outside. Imported birds (including those from Japan and Europe) are often especially delicate and should be kept indoors for the first twelve months in lightly heated accommodations.

Two broods per year are not unusual. The aviary must be roomy and preferably planted with a few low shrubs. The shelter must be well protected from dampness and drafts. During long spells of dry weather, it is wise to lightly mist-spray the nest boxes on a daily basis so that the eggs do not desiccate. After the second brood has fledged, the nest box should be removed to stop the hen from laying again. Too many broods per season are unhealthy and could result in, among other things, egg binding. Later in the year, we must see that adults and youngsters are locked into the shelter at night. Cold nights are unhealthy for the youngsters because they tend to molt in the winter and so, for the first year, should be kept in lightly heated accommodations.

Turquioses are somewhat aggressive in the breeding season and each pair requires its own aviary. On reaching independence, juveniles also must be separated from the parents as the father can attack them with dire consequences. If the father should get too aggressive towards his young before they are independent, the young can be placed in an adjoining flight and the parents can then feed them through the mesh. Typically, a cock will worry his sons but leave his daughters in peace. Young birds can be extremely nervous and panicky, making it necessary to cover the inner aviary mesh with twigs so that they don't injure themselves on the wire; after a couple of weeks, the twigs can be removed. In general, I would recommend the minimum of nest inspections, but some are essential in that the hen sometimes will lay her second clutch before the young from the first have left the nest. Captive hybrids with *Neophema splendida, N. elegans,* and *N. chrysostoma* have been produced.

Mutations: A number of mutations are well known: yellow-pied, olive-green, yellow, and fallow; in addition there have been reports of blue, opaline and lutino mutations. The red-bellied turquoise is a special case and really is not a mutation. It also occurs in the wild. Selective breeding can intensify and increase the red color (possible through pairing together those birds with the most red coloring). As per Gloger's law, geographical subspecies from moist areas have a greater formation of melanine pigment than those from drier areas; in other words: the wetter the habitat, the redder the bird, the drier the habitat, the yellower the bird. This can mean that those from wet areas have a better chance of breeding redder birds than those from dry areas. This phenomenon applies also to other *Neophema* species. An important feature of the yellow-pied mutation is that the red shoulder patch of the male is not always clearly discernable. This mutation is geneticaly sex-linked recessive.

The olive-green mutation first appeared in Denmark in 1980, but we have no further information. The beautiful yellow mutation however, is much better known, although I am not too happy with the description "yellow," and would rather, going by the color, call it pastel or light yellow-green. It is autosomal recessive in character and we therefore can expect to find split males and split females.

The fallow mutation is a somewhat pale colored bird with red eyes; the general impression is gray-green. This mutation is also autosomal recessive in character.

The "real" blue mutation is (to date) not yet bred, but the pastel blue has. The underside of this bird is creamish; and the back is sea-green. It is also an autosomal recessive mutation. The opaline, first bred in Germany, has a deep yellow mantel, head, and back. It is a sex-linked recessive mutation. The lutino also originated in Germany; what was blue became white. They are still very scarce, but because they are so beautiful breeders will ensure that we will soon see more of them.

The Species

Blue-winged Grass Parakeet— *Neophema chrysostoma*

chrysostoma: golden beak.

Neophema chrysostoma. The blue-winged grass parakeet is well known for its adaptability, especially regarding food. Its main diet in the wild consists of various grass and herbaceous seeds, taken on the ground, freshly sown oats, berries, and on occasion, insects.

Description: The cock is mainly green in color. This is darker on the shoulders and back, but goes over to greenish yellow on the belly. Lores are orange-yellow. The wings are mainly blue; innermost tail feathers are light orange-yellow. There is a blue forehead band that reaches the eye (in the elegant parakeet, which is similar in color, this stripe continues behind the eye). There is an orange-pink patch on the belly. The hen is generally duller in color and the blue is diluted with yellowish-green tints; the forehead band is smaller; the flight feathers are brown (black in the male). The eyes are brown, the beak is bluish-gray, the feet are brownish-gray. The young do not have the blue forehead stripe or only a faint sign of it. The blue in the wings is also barely apparent. The young reach full color in about eight months and are sexually mature at one year of age.

Size: 8⅓ inches (21 cm) including the 4-inch (10-cm) long tail. Weight: cock, 1⅔ to 2 ounces (48–60 g); hen, 1½ to 1¾ ounces (44–50 g). Leg band: ¹¹⁄₆₄ inch (4 mm).

Voice: A soft and pleasant twittering. If alarmed, they emit a high and sharp two-toned whistle ("sit-sit"). While foraging, they emit a continual chattering.

Nest: In a hollow limb or trunk. The hen lays four to six white, almost spherical ⅞ by ¾ inch (22 x 19 mm) eggs that hatch in 18 to 19 days. The cock feeds the hen both inside and outside the nest. He also feeds the young after about one week. The young leave the nest at about three weeks of age and stay with their parents for a while. A second brood can then follow.

Distribution: Found in the western part of New South Wales, Victoria, and the southern part of South Australia as well as King Island and Tasmania. These beautiful birds are found in all kinds of habitats and are also common in European and American aviculture. In Tasmania they are commonly seen as winter migrants. The habits are similar to those of the elegant parakeet (see page 86).

Remarks: This species responds well to good husbandry, soon becoming tame and trusting. It is suitable for a community aviary at least 10 feet (3 m) in length. In the wild, these birds live in pairs or small groups, often accompanying other species such as the swift parakeet and the yellow-bellied rosella. My wife and I found eight separate nests of the blue-winged parakeet in abandoned owl nests! At other times, they are found in the abandoned nests of starlings or swallows. In captivity, the birds are fond of sweet, soft apples (in my experience wild specimens seldom take fruit). They also should be fed on grass and herb seeds, low-fat milk-soaked, stale, white bread (especially in the breeding season), canary grass seed, millet and millet sprays, a

The Species

little hemp, oats, crushed corn, and small or crushed sunflower seeds. Also, a little animal protein will not be amiss, especially in the breeding season. In the wild, this species also takes insects and other small invertebrates.

It seems that these birds do better if given a nest box that is not too small. One that is 15¾ inches (40 cm) deep and 8 by 8 inches (20 x 20 cm) in area is the minimum acceptable size. the entrance hole should be 2 to 2¾ inches (5–7 cm) in diameter. A piece of rope, bark, or cork should be affixed just below the nest opening, so that the hen can spend (as she is apt to) much time hanging on the box and inspecting the interior. The species has been crossed successfully with the elegant and turquoisine parakeets many times.

Elegant Grass Parakeet— *Neophema elegans*

elegans: elegant.

Neophema elegans. Recently the elegant grass parakeet appears to be the most plentiful of all *Neophema* species in the wild. In 1925, however, an aviculturist wrote that it needed to be saved from extinction.

Description: The cock is mainly yellowish green, lighter on the breast and underside of the tail. The lores, throat, and forepart of the cheeks are bright yellow, and there is a narrow, blue forehead band. The wing feathers are edged in blue and there are a few orange feathers on the lower belly. The back is olive-green and the flight feathers are blackish-blue. The hen is less yellowish and has no orange feathers on the belly (occasionally she may have a few but these usually are lost after a few molts). The flight feathers are brown with lighter edges. On fledging, young males already are brighter in color than the females and only the forehead band is undeveloped. In six months, the juvenile molt usually is over and the birds have full adult plumage. They are sexually mature in twelve months.

Size: 9 inches (23 cm) including the 4⅓-inch (11 cm) long tail. Weight: cock, 1½ to 1¾ ounces (42–51 g); hen, 1½ ounces (42–44 g). Leg band: ¹¹⁄₆₄ inch (4 mm).

Voice: A sharp "tseet-tseet-tseet…tseet-tseet-tseet" uttered mainly in flight. During feeding, the birds chatter in a sharp tone interspersed with shrill shreaks.

Nest: In a tree hollow (in captivity they require a nest box 6 by 6 by 11¾ inches (15 x 15 x 30 cm) with an entrance hole 5 cm in diameter). The hen lays four to five white, round eggs ⁵³⁄₆₄ by ²³⁄₃₂ inch (21 x 18 mm) eggs on a layer of mulch or earth. The hen incubates alone for 18 days, and after a further four weeks the young leave the nest. The young remain in close contact with the parents until they themselves are ready to reproduce.

Distribution: Found in the southern part of New South Wales, western Victoria, South Australia (north to the Flinders Ranges), and southwestern Australia (north to Moora and east to Esperance). This species lives mainly on sparsely treed grassland, agricultural areas, parks, and gardens. They live in pairs or small groups. They follow human habitation and turn up wherever woodland has been cleared; they even have occurred as far north as the

Pilbara district…thus into the tropics. They also are common along the coast; we often have seen them early in the morning flying high in the sky like larks.

Remarks: Research has shown that this species is increasing in the wild and occurs in most kinds of open country. Groups of 20 to 100 birds are not at all uncommon, and only in the breeding season do they disperse into pairs or small groups. Sometimes they may be seen in the company of blue-winged grass parakeets, which are similar in appearance and life-style. The elegant can be distinguished by its yellow-green breast, the light-blue forehead band that stretches above and behind the eyes, and less blue on the wings than the blue-wing. Foraging mainly on the ground, they eat much seed (especially from *Paspalum* grass), and fruit, berries, and other vegetable food. When alarmed, the birds first sit stock-still on a twig and do not fly off until the last moment in search of a safer tree or clump of bushes near the ground. Their flight is fast and (especially in open situations) they will fly high in the air to avoid predatory birds. Captive care is similar to that described for Bourke's parakeet (see page 00). Crossings with *N. pulchella*, *N. splendida*, and *N. chrysostoma* are not uncommon in our aviaries.

Mutations: Among others, the yellow pied, the pastel green, the cinnamon, and the lutino mutations occur. The yellow pied is dominant in character, so that pied young can arise from a pairing with a normal bird. There are no "split" birds. It is an uncommon mutation.

The pastel green and the cinnamon are also rare, and the genetic makeups are respectively autosomal recessive and sex-linked recessive. The lutino has been known for much longer than the other mutations; it is silver-yellow with red eyes and white feathers where they are blue in the normal. Contrary to most lutinos, this form of the elegant is not sex-linked but autosomal recessive in character. Both sexes can thus be split for lutino.

Splendid Grass Parakeet— *Neophema splendida*

splendida: beautiful, splendid.

Neophema splendida. The splendid or scarlet-chested grass parakeet is unfortunately a rare species in the wild, possibly due to its quiet and secretive habits.

Description: The cock has a sea-blue head and neck; the upper side is green, the underside is yellow with a red breast; the wings are bluish-green with lighter blue and black. The tail is green with yellow and black. The eyes are brown, the feet are brownish-black, and the beak is black. The hen has a yellowish-green underside; the breast has an olive-green tinge, the back is darker than in the cock. The sides of the head are less blue; the red breast is missing. The youngsters are similar in appearance to the hen, but somewhat duller. Only the blue on the head is somewhat more intensive in young males.

Size: 8 inches (20 cm) including the 3½-inch (9-cm) long tail. Weight: male, 1½ ounces (40–44 g); female, 1¼ ounces (36–37 g). Leg band: ¹¹⁄₆₄ inch (4 mm).

The Species

Voice: A soft, pleasant, ringing whistle.

Nest: Usually in a hollow limb of an acacia or eucalyptus tree. The hen lays two to six round, white eggs $^{29}/_{32}$ by ¾ inch (23 x 19 mm) eggs deposited on a bed of mulch or wood splinters. The incubation period is 18 days and the cock feeds the hen both outside and inside the nest. He also helps feed the young after they are about ten days old. The younsters fledge after about four weeks and are very nervous in the first few days.

Distribution: Found in western New South Wales, through the northern part of South Australia to near the coast at the Great Australian Bight, and landwards into Western Australia. This species is fairly nomadic and can be seen in varied habitats, including acacia scrub. I have seen birds many miles from water and have since discovered that this is a normal phenomenon. Indeed; the species is steadily moving inland and is increasing in numbers year by year in southwestern Australia.

Remarks: It is quite remarkable that this species was more or less undetected for a hundred years; it was first "rediscovered" in 1941 in Western Australia. Observations have shown that this beautiful, slender species is very peaceful and has a somewhat secretive life-style. Whenever I approached them in the wild, they stood stock-still in the undergrowth become virtually invisible. The terrain in which the birds usually occur is mainly grassland (mulga and spinifex, for example) and small groups will stay in a certain area as long as food and water is available, moving on when necessary. However, due to the climatic changes in these arid areas, the birds usually are on the move continually. The splendid grass parakeet is not too fearful of humans, and those that live near habitations will show themselves "bold as brass." Many times I been able to approach them closely in parks and gardens. The soft chatter is pleasant to listen to and in no way nerve splitting, like the voices of many other psittacines. They do not drink much; we have seen them in waterless areas for several days where my wife and I had set up camp.

Although not common in captivity, once one has a true pair they will breed readily; care is similar to that described for the other *Neophema* species. Dr. Immelman states that according to ornithologist Y.A. Pepper, the hens of the splendid parakeet in Western Australia line their nest hollows with leaves and other soft material. They bite the leaves from the twigs and tuck them under the rump feathers for transportation. This remarkable behavior is otherwise only exhibited by the lovebirds of the family *Agapornidae.*

Mutations: The mutations of the splendid parakeet include yellow-pied, sea-green, pastel-blue, blue, cinnamon, isabel, fallow, and red-bellied. The pied version has a number of green feathers replaced by yellow and a number of blue feathers replaced by white—in both cases the blue is missing. The pied mutation is dominant in character. Fledglings are not pied; this arises with the first molt.

The sea-green, pastel-blue, and blue together form the "blue series" in which the yellow is diminished and the blue intensified. The blue is sometimes called the white-breasted blue; this is confusing as it is really a silver-blue mutation; in such a case the colors yellow and red are lost so that the male's breast becomes white. In the other two, a little (diluted) red remains. The genetical character of all three is autosomal recessive.

The isabel and the cinnamon are similar to each other. The back color of the cinnamon is said to be "yellowish moss-green," whereas that of the isabel is somewhat lighter than the wild color. The clearest difference is to be seen in the flight feathers; in the cinnamon we have beige tints, whereas in the isabel these are brown-gray. In addition, the blue in the cinnamon is a little duller. Both are sex-linked recessive in genetical makeup.

The fallow can be described as a somewhat paler version of the wild color with dark red eyes. The colors are somewhat matt, the character is autosomal recessive.

The dark green is a darker version of the wild

color, thus in the "green-series" with a dark factor; the mauve is in the "blue-series" with two dark factors.

The same applies to the red-belly as to the red-bellied turquoisine; this is developed through selective breeding, it is somewhat lighter in shade than the breast color.

Just like mutations in other birds, further colors can be developed by breeding combinations of the above mutations. Examples include the silver splendid (from cinnamon x blue) and the sky-blue splendid (from isabel x blue).

Bourke's Parakeet—*Neophema bourkii*

bourkii: after Fort Bourke, from which Thomas Livingstone Mitchell (1792–1855) left on expeditions and discovered this species in 1838. Sir Richard Bourke was a governor of the Australian state of New South Wales.

Description: It is pinkish, checked with dark brown. The crown, neck, back, wings, and tail are chestnut brown. The edges of the wings (also inside) are blue, as are the lower tail feathers. It has a bluish-white eye stripe. The wing feathers are banded with white, the out flight feathers are bluish-white. The hen has a somewhat rounder head and most of the blue above the beak is missing. After nine, sometimes eight, months the young come into full color, but before this the sexes are difficult to distinguish. The eyes are brown, the beak is shiny black and the feet are light brown.

Size: 7½ inches (19 cm) including the 3½-inch (9-cm) long tail. Weight: cock, 1⅔ to 1¾ ounces (47–49 g); hen, 1½ to 1¾ ounces (41–49 g). Leg band: ¹¹⁄₆₄ inch (4 mm).

Voice: A frequently repeated (also while flying) mellow "chu- vee"; sometimes a hard and penetrating, rolling whistle ending in a soft, pleasant whistle.

Nest: In small tree hollows, especially in acacia and casuarina, to 10 feet (3 m) above the ground.

Neophema bourkii. In the wild, Bourke's parakeets fly about on moonlit nights, and are active at dusk. In times of drought, they often can be seen in large numbers at watering places, although they usually operate in pairs or small family groups.

The hen lays three to six white, roundish ²⁵⁄₃₂ by ²¹⁄₃₂ inches (20 x 17 mm) eggs on a layer of wood pulp. The hen incubates alone for 18 days, and the cock feeds her on the nest.

Distribution: From the southwestern part of Queensland and deep into western New South Wales through central Australia to the far north of South Australia and parts of the inland of Western Australia. Due to the clearing of many water holes, this species is decreasing alarmingly in numbers. Being nomadic, the birds probably are more abundant than is apparent. They live in pairs or small groups (families), but during times of prolonged drought they may gather together in hundreds or more. The birds are quiet and peaceful, also in the wild, and their soft twittering in no way can be called unpleasant. Many naturalists have observed these birds at water holes very late in the evenings.

The Species

Remarks: Most available birds are captive bred; wild specimens are only available as contraband! In addition to the normal parakeet seed menu, they may be given hard-boiled egg and biscuits, a variety of green food, fresh twigs, and buds. They start to breed early in the year, so one must beware of egg binding. A pair can rear two or three broods per season. During the breeding season provide them with ants' eggs, small mealworms, rolled oats, a little hemp, crushed corn, small sunflower seeds, and a little fruit (if they will eat it, many individuals will not). As the birds are very peaceful, they can be kept in a community aviary with finches, doves, and other small parakeet species; but one pair per aviary is better. They must have a roomy flight, as they like to fly a lot. Many fanciers seed the floor of the flight so that the birds can forage in the grass. The nest box is 6 by 6 by 12 inches (15 x 15 x 30 cm) deep—entrance hole diameter 2 inches (5 cm)—also can have a layer of turf on the bottom. Always give the birds a choice of two or three nest boxes.

Mutations: At the present time, there are four documented Bourke's mutations: yellow, isabel, fallow, and pink. The yellow Bourke has a soft yellow back and wings; the head and breast are dull pink. The nails are very light as though illuminated. The cock is somewhat darker than the hen; the latter appearing yellower. The genetical character is autosomal recessive.

The isabel is similar to the yellow, but shows more pink and less yellow—going more towards brown. The feet and claws are more grayish. The eyes are red, like those of the yellow. The genetical character is sex-linked recessive. The fallow also belongs to the "yellow-series." It is similar to the isabel, but somewhat duller in color. The eyes are also red. The fallow has an off-white beak, the isabel's is more horn colored. The fallow is an autosomal recessive mutation. The rose Bourke is, in fact, an opaline mutation. It shows much variation in the pink. It is sex-linked recessive in character.

Swift Parakeet—*Lathamus discolor*

Lathamus: after Dr. John Latham (1740–1837), a famous eighteenth century British ornithologist; *discolor:* many colors, pied.

Lathamus discolor. In the wild, the swift parakeet migrates from Tasmania to the mainland, but breeds from about October to November only in Tasmania and on some islands in Bass Strait. The species is rather quiet, hardy, and amiable.

Description: Both sexes are similar in color and pattern, though the cock is somewhat more intensive. This bird has some lorikeet characteristics (climbs like a lorikeet and has a long, brush-tipped tongue like that of a lorikeet for collecting nectar, and so on) and is mainly green in color, with a bluish-purple crown, a red face, and pale blue cheeks. The face is bordered with yellow. There is a little red in the wings. The wing and tail feathers are dark purple-black. The shoulders, under tail coverts, and most of the small wing coverts are red. The eyes are pale yellow, the beak is horn colored, and the feet are brown. Young birds are duller in color and have less red on the throat and below the tail. The eyes are still brown.

Size: 9¾ inches (25 cm), including the 4¾-inch (12-cm) long tail. Weight: 1¾ to 2⅔ ounces (50–75 g). Leg band: ¹³⁄₆₄ inch (5 mm).

Voice: A metallic, high-pitched contact call ("klink, klink") quickly repeated four or five times. While feeding, they twitter constantly, making a flute-like sound.

Nest: In a hollow tree trunk, usually a eucalyptus. The hen lays three to five but usually four white ⁶³⁄₆₄ by ⁵¹⁄₆₄ inch (25 x 20 mm) eggs on a layer of wood splinters. Incubation by the hen takes 20 days and the cock feeds her during this time. Interestingly, in the wild several nests may be found in close proximity—even in the same tree. In captivity they must have a nest box 7 by 7 by 13¾ inches (18 x 18 x 35 cm) with an entrance hole 2⅓ inches (5.5 cm) in diameter.

Distribution: Found in southeastern Australia and Tasmania is wooded regions with flowers and blossoming trees. The bird breeds in Tasmania, but migrates thereafter to the mainland.

Remarks: They live mainly in the upper tree canopy leading a tumultuous existence, being very quick, active, and agile; they hang upside down to get at the nectar in the blossoms of trees. Sometimes their plumage becomes quite sticky from the nectar. These parakeets have a similar diet to the lorikeets and a lorikeet menu in captivity will be acepted; but one should not leave out the fruits, berries, smaller seeds, and a variety of green food. It is interesting to note that during the breeding time the hen is almost completely dependent on the cock. At feeding time, he calls her from the nest. In the wild, the hen flies usually to a branch close by and, after being fed by the cock, climbs back to the nest. In the aviary it is therefore recommended that a number of (natural) perches are placed around the nest box. A flight that is 12 feet (3.5 m) long is ideal; the birds are not aggressive, but extremely active. Twigs with blossoms can be given as an extra food supplement. This species is strong in constitution and not

difficult to overwinter in an outdoor aviary providing a draft- and damp-proof night shelter is available. The swift parakeet soon becomes tame and is very fond of a water bath.

Mutations: There is a yellow mutation, though the color is more yellowish-green than pure yellow, with a matt blue head. This is sex-linked recessive in character.

Red- or Crimson-winged Parakeet—*Aprosmictus erythropterus*

Aprosmictus: not mixed with others, isolated; *erythropterus:* red wings; *coccineopterus:* scarlet wings.

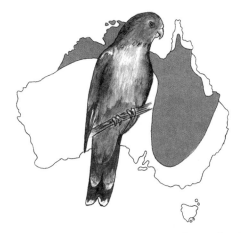

Aprosmictus erythropterus. The red- or crimson-winged parakeet usually operates in pairs or family groups, and is mostly arboreal. At adequate food sources, the species may even be seen in large flocks.

Description: The male is mainly green in color with some blue tones at the back of the head. The shoulders and upper back are black, the rest of the back is blue, paler close to the rump. The wing coverts are red, the primaries are mainly dark green. The rest of the wing and the tail is also green, the latter with vague yellow tips to the feathers. The eyes are orange-red, the beak is coral red, and the feet are gray. The hen is dull green with a yellow-green underside and has only a small amount of red in the wing coverts. The lowest part of the back and the rump are bluish. The eyes are pale brown. Young birds are, at first, very similar to the hen apart from the darker eye color. The sex can be determined by the color of the rump, which is more intensive blue in the male. However, one can be more sure at eighteen months of age when the males start to get their black feathers on the back. Some breeders have a little trick—by pulling out a few back feathers, these will be replaced by black in the male, green with a female. The development of adult plumage occurs much later than even with the King parakeet *(Alisturus scapularis)*. They are fully colored at two and one-half years and, in the wild they breed in their third year.

Size: 12½ inches (32 cm). Weight: male, 4¼ to 5 ounces (120–146 g); female, 5¼ ounces (149 g). Leg band: ¼ inch (6 mm).

Voice: A brassy "krillik, krillik" used as a contact call. During feeding they utter a constant soft twittering.

Nest: In a hollow tree trunk, close to water. The nest hole is deep and the floor lined with a layer of wood pulp and splinters. The hen lays five or six about 1¼ by 1 inch (31 x 26 mm) eggs. She incubates alone and the eggs hatch in about 20 days. Both parents feed the young, which fledge at about 35–40 days.

Distribution: Found in the greater part of northern and northeastern Australia and also in southern New Guinea. There are three subspecies: *A. e. erythropterus* (from eastern Australia), the smaller and duller colored *A. e. coccineopterus* (from northern Australia and some adjacent islands and further in western "parrotland"), and *A. e. papua* from New Guinea. These parakeets live in pairs or small groups (up to 60 birds in food-rich territory). They feed on flowers, nectar, fruit, nuts, seeds, and insects.

Remarks: At mating time, the male circles in the air and lands on a twig close to his prospective bride; he lets his wings droop and shows the blue on his back. Next, he pulls in all his feathers tightly and walks close to his partner, making several passes. In the aviary they are very quiet and peaceful birds, but they like to use their wings so they must have a roomy flight. These birds spend more time in the tree foliage than on the ground, so food should be offered on a tray at least 3 feet (1 m) from the floor. Once acclimatized, these birds are hardy but should be housed indoors during the winter in our colder states. Such indoor accommodations require no heating, but must be well lit. The birds can be fussy in their choice of partner, so a shuffling of birds among fellow fanciers may be required in order to produce compatible pairs. Feed on canary grass seed, sunflower seeds, oats, crushed corn, fruit, berries, almonds, peanuts, and raisins. Do not forget an adequate variety of green food; stale bread or sponge cake soaked in low-fat milk or water, but only enough of the latter for them to eat at one sitting (it quickly spoils). These birds also sometimes will take mealworms and ants' eggs to feed their young. A grandfather clock-type nest box should be supplied, this being 7 feet (2 m) deep and 13¾ x 13¾ inches (35 x 35 cm) in floor area with a 3½ inch (9 cm) diameter entrance hole. The cock can become aggressive towards his hen during the breeding season so that some fanciers clip some of his flight feathers away, making him less agile so the hen can get away easily. Once independent, youngsters should be separated from their parents. Many hybrids are possible including with *Alisterus amboinensis sulaensis, A. scapularis, Polytelis alexandrae, P. anthopeplus, P. swainsonii,* and *Aprosmictus jonquillaceus.* New Guinea species may be available to the fancier; these are similar to the Australian type and the hen is barely distinguishable from *Aprosmictus erythropterus coccineopterus.*

This species requires an aviary at least 23 feet (7.5 m) long. In Arizona, a fancier bred successfully

The Species

from six pairs in one and the same aviary, 27 by 14 by 9 feet (9 x 4.5 x 2.7 m)! Red-winged parakeets are sensitive to frost and are susceptible to frostbite of the toes when claws and even bits of toe can be lost. The species also molts very early; earlier than most other Australian parakeets.

Mutations: There is a yellow-pied mutation.

Rock Pebbler Parakeet—*Polytelis anthopeplus*

Polytelis: very fine, noble, aristocratic; *anthopeplus:* feminine attire with flowers.

Polytelis anthopeplus. The young of the Rock pebbler parakeet are practically impossible to sex, and only after molt is completed are the bright yellow and red colors in the male clearly visible; the young birds are by then approximately 18 months old.

Description: The cock is mainly bright yellow in color with a touch of olive on the crown and neck. The wing coverts and primary flight feathers are dark, bluish-black; the secondary flight feathers are red; the tail is blue-black. The eyes are orange-brown, the beak is coral-red, and the feet are gray. The hen is much duller, being generally olive-green

with a lighter rump and leg feathers. The red in the wings is less obvious, and there is almost no yellow in the wings. Young birds are similar in appearance to the hen, but on fledging, the young males already are showing more yellow than the females; after 14–18 months, the young get their full adult plumage.

Size: 15¾ inches (40 cm), including the 8-inch (20-cm) long tail. Weight: male, 6 ounces (170 g); female, 6⅛ ounces (175 g). Leg band: ¹⁵⁄₆₄ inch (6 mm).

Voice: See the following species; the call is only louder and sharper in tone. During flight, these birds emit a loud, harsh "currac-currac."

Nest: In a hollow trunk or limb, the nest hole sometimes is more than 16 feet (5 m) down inside the tree. I also have found nests in rock crevices close to the river Murray.

Distribution: Found in southwestern Australia, in well-treed areas; much rarer in southeastern Australia. This species avoids humans wherever possible and rarely is seen in inhabited areas.

Remarks: These birds, fast on the wing, are like drops of gold. Once seen, they are an unforgetable sight as they fly around in pairs or small groups, resting in the early hours of the morning in the tops of trees where, with the blue background of the sky, they appear as golden jewels in the rays of the rising sun. In southwestern Australia, they frequently are seen in groups of 100 or more. During the breeding period, the cock feeds the hen on her nest. Care and management is similar to that described for the following species *(Barraband).* Crossings with *P. alexandrae, P. swainsonii,* and *Aprosmictus erythopterus* are known.

Barraband Parakeet—*Polytelis swainsonii*

swainsonii: William Swainson (1789–1855), an English ornithologist who first described the bird and named it after Jacques Barraband, a French ornithologist and bird painter.

The Species

Polytelis swainsonii. The Barraband's or Superb parakeet lives in a restricted range, although even in the early 1970s this brightly colored, elegantly formed species was still reported as far east as the Sydney area!

Description: The male is largely light green in color; the forehead, cheeks, and throat are canary yellow and separated from the breast with a red band. Coverts and primaries are dull blue. The tail is green above, and black beneath. The eyes are yellow/orange, the beak is coral-red, and the feet are gray. The hen is mainly dull green in color, with red in the thigh feathers. The young are similar in appearance to the hen, and first have brown eyes.

Size: 15¾ inches (40 cm), including the 10¼-inch (26-cm) long tail. Weight: male, 4⅔ to 5½ ounces (132–158 g); female, 5⅛ to 5½ ounces (145–155 g). Leg band: ¹⁵⁄₆₄ inch (6 mm).

Voice: A long held whistle, similar to that of the cockatiel, but ending more abruptly, it is also deeper and does not upturn at the end. This call is emitted continually, also when the birds are flying.

Nest: In a hollow tree trunk, often very high and out of reach of man and animal. The four to six white, roundish eggs are about 1 by ²⁹⁄₃₂ inch (28 x 24 mm) and are incubated for about 20 days. The young leave the nest at about four weeks. At six to nine months, they have adult plumage and are sexually mature at two years.

Distribution: They are found mainly along water courses in two main areas: the area around and along the rivers Castlereagh and Namoi, and the region around the rivers Murray, Murrumbidgee, and Lachlan (northern and southern New South Wales). In these relatively small areas, this species is quite common and somewhat nomadic as they feed largely on the blossoms of eucalyptus trees.

Remarks: They live in pairs or small groups and frequently seek eucalyptus seeds on the ground; they also take blossoms, pollen, nectar, fruit, nuts, grains, and so on. They often fly high in the air as they change feeding sites. In the breeding season, the cock flies above his chosen one and nods his head. The crown feathers can be raised in a mini-crest, which is done when the male approaches his partner perched on a branch chattering away and trying to impress his "bride to be." A receptive hen will sink "to her knees" and also raise a mini-crest, spread her wings, and emit a soft warbling tone (like that emitted by the young). The cock will then feed her with food he has brought. During breeding, he will continue to feed her in the nest. She incubates alone, but the cock helps feeding the young after about their tenth day. During the first ten days, he feeds the hen alone and she passes some of the food on to the young. The young leave the nest at about five weeks of age. It is about six months before the young males start developing their adult plumage and two or three months more before they are in full adult plumage. In captivity they must have a roomy aviary as they are very active on the wing. They feed on sunflower seeds, oats, wheat, crushed corn, canary grass seed, sorghum, and millet plus fruit and berries, various nuts, raisins, and willow and fruit tree twigs. Milk-soaked, stale white bread may be given, especially in the breeding season. These birds like to bathe and must be offered daily facilities for this. A large nest box of the grandfather clock type or a deep, hollow log should be given; it is best to give them a choice for optimum results. Crossings with *Alisterus scapularis, Aprosmictus erythropterus,* and *Platycercus eximius* have been successful several times, though personally I do not approve of such hybrids and am more for keeping the species and races pure.

Princess of Wales Parakeet—
Polytelis alexandrae

alexandrae: In 1863, the ornithlogist John Gould named this species after Princess Alexandra, daughter of the King of Denmark and married to the Prince of Wales. Both later became King (Edward VII) and Queen of England.

Polytelis alexandrae. The Princess of Wales parakeet is nomadic, and an inhabitant of the far inland. The bird usually frequents timber belts along or near water courses. It occasionally has the strangely reptilian habit of lying or sitting *along* tree branches rather than *across* them.

Description: The crown and nape are pastel blue. The forehead and sides of the head are pale blue-gray; the cheek, throat, and most of the breast are pink. It has an olive-yellow mantle, back, and wings. The wing coverts are yellow, below is blue. Central tail feathers are olive-green, the outers are edged with blue-gray. The flanks are pink and blue, lower tail coverts are olive-yellow, and the rump is violet-blue. The cock also has an extension of the third, primary flight feathers; known as the spatula. The eyes are orange, the beak is coral red, and the feet are gray. The hen has a grayish-mauve crown; the back and rump are grayish blue. All the other colors are duller. The central tail feathers are shorter than in the cock. Young birds are strongly similar to the hen.

Size: 17¾ inches (45 cm) including the 11-inch (28-cm) long tail. Weight: 3⅛ to 3⅓ ounces (90–94 g). Leg band: ¹⁵⁄₆₄ inch (6 mm).

Voice: A somewhat rattling call, nothing like the call of a parrot or parakeet but more like the call of an Australian kingfisher. When resting in the trees, the birds emit an almost continuous chattering; alarm call is a quick "queen-queen."

Nest: In a hollow limb, close to water and usually in a eucalyptus (occasionally in a casuarina tree far from water). The hen lays four to six, shiny-white, roundish eggs, about 1 by ⅞ inch (26 x 22 mm).

Distribution: Found in the arid, desert areas of central and Western Australia.

Remarks: This species is very scarce (according to the *Atlas of Australian Birds,* it was last seen in 1981) and nomadic. They usually live in small groups (15–20 birds). Courtship is like that of the preceding species. Young cocks are in full color by fifteen to eighteen months of age. The hen incubates the eggs alone for 20 days. The young leave the nest at five weeks but stay with their parents for some time thereafter. When danger threatens, these birds fly into a tree and crouch horizontally along a branch so that they are difficult to detect. These really stunning birds are bred regularly in captivity.

The Species

They require a spacious aviary (minimum length 12 feet (3.5 m)) in which they will fly about regularly. As the cocks can be somewhat argumentative, it is best to keep each pair separately. These birds are usually most active mornings and evenings and forage on the ground in search of seeds, insects and their larvae and so on. For the rest of the day, they can sit with their heads tucked under the wings, but not all birds behave like this.

A nest box, 23⅔ by 8 by 8 inches (60 x 20 x 20 cm) with an entrance hole 2¾ inches (7 cm) in diameter is ideal. The box can be fixed in a slanting poition so that the hen can walk to the eggs and not fall on them. Sometimes the males have a leaning towards "playing football" with the eggs. If you see such behavior, you can remove the male for a time or you can make the entrance hole smaller with a piece of bark, for example. The hen will then gnaw the hole to her own size and keep the more robust cock outside. One also can replace the eggs with artificial ones, putting the real eggs back when the hen begins to seriously incubate. Unlike the other two members of the genus, this species is more susceptible to eye infections.

Mutations: There are blue, lutino, and albino mutations, all of which are autosomal recessive in character. Albinos can be produced by crossing lutino and blue.

Red-capped Parakeet— *Purpureicephalus spurius*

Purpureicephalus: purple head; *spurius:* false, artificial.

Description: The crown is red; the back of the neck is green; the rest of the head is yellow. It has a blue breast and belly, red thigh feathers and ventral tail coverts, a yellow rump, and green wings with sky-blue and dark blue flight feathers. The eyes are dark brown, the beak is bluish-gray; and the feet are brown. The hen is duller in color and greener (frequently also on the crown), her breast is gray-

Purpureicephalus spurius. The elongated upper mandible of the hardy, quiet but nervous red-capped parakeet is extremely well suited for extracting the seeds of the eucalyptus.

mauve. The young have a green crown and nape and a rust-colored band on the forehead. At first all the colors are pale.

Size: 14⅛ inches (36 cm) including the 7-inch (18-cm) long tail. Weight: male, 3⅔ to 5½ ounces (104–157 g); female, 3½ to 4¾ ounces (98–135 g). Leg band: ¹⁵⁄₆₄ inch (6 mm).

Voice: A grating kurr-kurr-uk repeated several times, especially when on the wing. A loud shriek as an alarm call. No chattering while feeding.

Nest: In a hollow tree, especially the marri (*Eucalyptus calophylla);* the entrance hole usually is high up. The hen lays four to seven but usually five round, white eggs, about 1 by ²⁹⁄₃₂ inch (26 x 23 mm) on a bed of wood chips. The hen incubates alone for about 20 days before the young hatch. These fledge at about five weeks. Young cocks are almost in full color at fifteen months. Hens are usually not in adult color until the second molt. Although they stay with the parents in the wild for a year or more, it is best to remove independent aviary young from the parents as the father can get aggressive towards them.

Distribution: Found in southwestern Australia. They live chiefly in areas wooded with marri trees in which they nest and feed on the seeds. It is atrocious that most of these trees (which have very little, if any, commercial value) are being felled in favor of trees with a greater commercial value, or to make agricultural or residential areas—thus destroying the habitat of these birds and other animals, resulting in their serious decline. Unless immediate and positive action is taken by the responsible state and federal governments in Australia, it may be too late to save this beautiful, colorful parakeet. The bird also occurs in plantations and parks (especially around Perth).

Remarks: These are peaceful birds and enthusiastic bathers that feed the same as many lorikeets and the swift parakeet. In spring and summer, they frequently descend to the ground to eat grass seeds and similar food. In the aviary they can be quite nervous, especially when first placed in new accommodations; any glass should be covered with twigs so the birds do not fly into it and kill themselves. Other obstacles, such as feeding platforms, should be removed at first for safety's sake. Some shrubs planted around the aviary will be useful in helping to calm the birds.

Red-capped parakeets are accomplished gnawers and can soon damage the structure of a wooden aviary with their strong beaks. Exposed timber therefore should be covered with sheet metal. Give the birds an adequate supply of twigs and branches to keep them occupied. As well as green food and fruit, give them a mixture of canary grass seed, sunflower seed and oats (in a ratio of 2:1:1), and especially the berries of hawthorn. In the breeding season especially, milk-soaked bread or sponge cake with grape juice or honey will not go amiss. Breeding birds must be given utmost privacy! Give them a choice of large hollow logs or deep nest boxes 25 by 30 inches (65–75 cm) deep and 10 by

10 inches (25 x 25 cm) square—entrance hole 3 inches (7.5 cm) in diameter. Allow only one brood per year so that the young get full attention from their parents. Crossings with *Platycercus elegans, P. icterotis* and *P. caledonicus* are known.

Now to a further discussion on interspecific crossings. As true pairs of specific species may be hard to come by, breeders are tempted to try mating different species together, thus producing hybrids with characteristics of two species mixed together. If the hybrids are fertile, further crossings can result in "impure" strains of certain species and it becomes very difficult to "remold" a pure species once this has happened. Though it is interesting to make such crossings, I am of the opinion that we should be really doing our utmost in obtaining true pairs of a species and making it our duty to keep species pure. Over a period, one can be more successful with pure stock than with a mixture of hybrids—especially as it is now virtually impossible to get "fresh wild blood" to improve it.

The rosella *(Platycercus eximius)* can be crossed with the pale-headed rosella, the Stanley rosella, the Adelaide rosella, the pennant, and Brown's rosella. It also has been crossed with the Barnard's parakeet *(Barnardius barnardi)*, the Port Lincoln, *(Barnardius zonarius)*, the red-rump *(Psephotus haematonotus)*, the red-cap *(Purpureicephalus spurius)*, and the Barraband *(Polytelis swainsonii)*. Other crossings have occurred such as with the yellow-bellied rosella *(Platycercus caledonicus)*, but the young are not very attractive.

The pale-headed rosella *(Platycercus adscitus)* is a bird that seems to be particularly made for crossings! Some possibilities are with the eastern rosella (although the red is difficult to get back by re-pairing), the Stanley rosella, the pennant, and Brown's rosella; it also will cross with the red-rump and the Barnard.

In Australia, North America, and Europe, crossings of the Adelaide rosella with the yellow-headed rosella and pennant have been accomplished. Mr. Huckley Smith paired a hen Adelaide with a yellow-bellied rosella cock. This breeding also has occurred reversed.

The Stanley rosella, with its beautiful red coloration is also the "victim" of mixed pairings, especially with the eastern rosella, the pale-headed rosella, and the pennant. The yellow-bellied rosella can be crossed with the Adelaide, the Barnard, the port Lincoln, and similar.

The pennant has been crossed with the Adelaide, the yellow-bellied, the eastern, and the pale-headed rosellas. An interesting crossing is that with the pennant x ringneck parakeet *(Psittacula kramer krameri).* It also has been crossed with the Barnard and the Port Lincoln parakeets.

The yellow rosella can be paired successfully with the eastern rosella, the pennant, the Adelaide, the Barnard, and the red-rump. Finally, Brown's rosella has been paired with the yellow rosella in California and it also has crossed with the eastern rosella.

I am aware that, in this summary, I have not covered all cases, but I hope the above will give the reader some idea of the possibilities. It is important that we do our utmost to keep our animals (including birds) and plants in their original form. As mentioned above, it is very difficult (or impossible) to breed purity back into our parakeets once it has been lost. I think we are responsible for keeping our aviary birds as pure as possible.

Pennant or Crimson Rosella— *Platycercus elegans*

Platycercus: flat or broad tail; *elegans:* elegant; *nigrescens:* becoming black; *melanoptera:* black-winged; Pennant: Thomas Pennant was an important natural history writer around the 1800s.

Description: The pennant or crimson rosella is undoubtedly one of the most beautiful Australian parakeets. As it is a fairly easy captive breeder, pairs frequently are seen in large cages or aviaries. A

Platycercus elegans. The hardy pennant or crimson rosella is unsuitable for a mixed collection; each pair should be housed in its own aviary. For proper breeding results, limit nest inspections to the minimum.

good pair of these birds is therefore within the budget of most fanciers.

It is not easy to distinguish the cock from the hen. The birds have a sky-blue colored throat that runs through to the cheeks. The secondary wing feathers are also blue, with darker patches, whereas the primaries are purplish-blue. The main body color is a deep crimson or wine-red; the tail is blue. The back feathers are blackish, bordered with crimson. As the colors do not permit us to distinguish the sexes, we have to look at form. The male's head is larger and more flattened than that of the female.

A pair of elegant golden-shouldered parakeets, ▶ undoubtedly one of Australia's most colorful and also most threatened birds! In the wild, these birds live in lightly wooded country with functioning termite mounds in which they build their nests.

The Species

The beak is also larger in the male. Even immature youngsters can be sexed fairly easily by comparing head and beak sizes. Young birds are usually greenish in color, but there is no hard and fast rule and some birds have a reddish tinge. The full adult colors—beautiful blue and crimsom—appear after the molt when the birds are fifteen to eighteen months old. This "metamorphosis" is usually seen in the autumn. In both sexes, the back and part of the wings are "checked" in black. The eyes are dark-brown, the beak grayish-yellow, usually with a dark spot; the legs and feet are grayish-brown.

Size: 12⅔ to 14⅕ inches (32–36 cm); tail, 5½ to 6⅔ inches (14-17 cm). Weight: Male elegant, 4⅓ to 6 ounces (123–170 g); female, 4 to 5⅛ ounces (112–146 g). Male *nigrescens*, 4 to 4¼ ounces (112–120 g). Leg band: ¹⁵⁄₆₄ inch (6 mm).

Voice: see Yellow-bellied Rosella.

Nest: In a hollow tree limb, usually a eucalyptus. The clutch consists of four to eight, but usually five, eggs. They are creamy-white in color and almost globular about 1 by ⁶¹⁄₆₄ inch (29 x 24 mm). The hen broods the eggs for 21 days. After another five weeks, the young leave the nest but spend about another month in the company of their parents. The nest box should be approximately 9 by 9 inches (22 x 22 cm), with a height of 21 inches (55 cm) and an entrance hole of 2¾ inches (7 cm) diameter.

Distribution: Found in southern and eastern Australia. In the northeastern part of Queensland a darker variety occurs, the *Platycerus elegans nigrescens*, which is somewhat smaller than the type species but not separated from it. However, in the trade, it is often available under the name of pennant parakeet and the minor differences are ignored. The color differences are so small that only serious ornithologists are concerned with them. The subspecies *P. e. melanoptera*, which can be distinguished from others by its dark, almost black, back feathers, occurs on Kangaroo Island. *P. e. fleurieuensis* is found in the foothills of South Australia's Mount Lofty ranges.

Remarks: In the wild, the pennant inhabits rough, hilly grass and bushland. To the concern of farmers, it also occurs in agricultural areas. Unfortunately these birds, like many other Australian psittacines, are very destructive to crops and can destroy a whole harvest of corn, for example. Goverment schemes allow wholesale numbers of the birds to be culled. In suburban areas, the birds have become used to humans and they frequently visit gardens, where they are fed with leftovers and entertain the donors with their splendid coloration and their not unpleasant, chirping calls. These birds frequently nest in gardens and parks, even in suitable areas of the inner city. I have observed these birds take animal food, such as flies, larvae, caterpillars (but, as far as I am aware, not the hairy sort), as well as their staple diet of various seeds (mainly from eucalyptus).

The first pennants must have arrived in Europe around 1873 as a successful breeding was reported in the literature in 1874. In Belgium, in 1879, more birds were bred and it became apparent that the birds made splendid captives. With protection from rain and drafts, these birds can spend the winter in outdoor aviaries. Due to their destructiveness to timber, it is recommended that aviaries are constructed with metal frames or that any exposed timber is covered with sheet metal. Timber aviaries would be totally destroyed within a year, making them unsuitable even for nondestructive species.

Aviary breeding is not always easy. There seems to be a large number of bad hens among the captive stock, including egg peckers! But, with our present bird societies it should be possible to get a good, compatible pair together without too many problems. Adult birds frequently are aggressive and

◀ Top: Golden-shouldered parakeet nestlings. Due to the fact that young birds are rather thinly feathered, they require a special nest box. Bottom: Young perching golden-shouldered parakeets with their proud parents. With proper care and management the young will become extremely tame and affectionate.

each pair must be kept in its own accommodations. Even then, one should watch out for any aggressiveness from the cock to the hen. The birds are hardy and can withstand low temperatures. They also are very active and will spend much time rummaging on the aviary floor.

The rules of Gloger and Bergmann apply to pennants: those birds from warmer areas (subspecies *nigrescens*) are usually smaller than those from colder areas *(elegans)*; and those from wetter areas *(nigrescens)* are darker in color than those from drier climes *(elegans)*.

Mainly green or mainly red youngsters sometimes emerge from the nest boxes. These probably also occur in the wild. Experiments in Germany over many years have led to interesting results. One fancier removed some of the youngsters from the nest box for a few hours each day so that they received less food. Those left in the nest received food from the parents, plus extra food from the fancier. This was done with several broods and in every case, the poorly fed young became red, whereas the well fed birds became green. Thus, quantities of adequate food affect the feather color.

Mutations: Pennants occur in blue, yellow and white. There are also lutinos. The blue is fairly well established but the other mutations are still rare. The blue pennant cannot strictly be called blue, even though this color results from a deficiency of carotenoids. The red is replaced by a grayish color.

The white can be bred from a blue and a yellow. An albino can be bred from a blue and a lutino. Further details of color expectations are given in Heredity and Mutations (see Colors, pages 70–71).

The lutino keeps a red head, back, and breast, whereas the blue and black parts become white; the eyes are always red.

The blue, yellow, and white are autosomal recessive inheritances, the lutino probably sex-linked recessive though not definite as we usually regard lutinos as autosomal recessive.

Adelaide Rosella—*Platycercus elegans adelaidae*

With its soft coloring, the Adelaide rosella is undoubtedly one of the most beautiful subspecies of the pennant. Color differences among this subspecies are frequent, making it sometimes difficult to distinguish them from others. The predominantly red individuals resemble pennants, whereas those with more yellow are similar to the yellow rosella. The scientific name shows that the Adelaide rosella is closely related to the pennant. Many ornithologists are of the opinion that this bird arises as a result of a cross between a pennant and a yellow rosella.

The main colors are orange-red, with blue cheeks, tail, and wings. The center tail feathers are green with a blue sheen. The back feathers are black with red edges; in the hen, the edges are frequently yellowish-green or light red. The black shoulder patch, which occurs in all rosellas, is particularly conspicuous. It is difficult to make any hard and fast rules regarding determination of the sexes, as the colors vary so much. However the head of the cock is usually larger, squarer, and more robust than that

Platycercus elegans adelaidae. The Adelaide rosella, considered by many ornithologists as a transitional form (not a separate species), is a hardy aviary bird. The nest box should be placed in the open run.

of the hen. Young birds have more green in the plumage and get their full adult plumage at twelve to fourteen months. Adelaide, the beautiful capital city of South Australia, is situated precisely in the center of the native habitat of this rosella and the bird thus derives its name. I have observed these birds even in the suburbs of the town where, unfortunately, they can cause some damage, especially in nurseries and young plantations.

According to Condon and Keast, Adelaides come in four color varieties:
• the dark-red Adelaide, found in Queensland;
• the moderately dark-red Adelaide of New South Wales;
• the pale-red Adelaide, found in the immediate region of the South Australian capital, and
• the Kangaroo type, found on Kangaroo Island.

Various bird experts are of the opinion that the Adelaide rosella is a result of possible crossings between the pennant and the yellow rosellas; this opinion is based on the different color varieties of the Adelaides and the fact that pennants and yellows are found in the same areas as the Adelaides. Whatever the answer, the Adelaide is unfortunately not so common in our aviaries as the pennant.

It is interesting to note that spontaneous crossings between pennants and yellows do occur in the wild. In England, captive crossings have produced "instant" Adelaides; but really it is not quite as simple as that!

Size: 13¾ inches (35 cm); tail, 6⅓ to 6⅔ inches (16–17 cm). Weight: male, 4 to 5¾ ounces (112–165 g); female, 3½ to 5⅔ ounces (100–160 g). Leg band: ¹⁵⁄₆₄ inch (6mm).

Yellow Rosella—*Platycercus elegans flaveolus*

Also a variant of the pennant. It is a beautiful bird (*flaveolus* means becoming golden-yellow) but not the most colorful of the rosella group. The parakeet is mainly yellow in color (from which the name obviously arises), but with blue cheeks and blue wing bars. The outer tail feathers also have a

Platycercus elegans flaveolus. The attractive yellow rosella, which usually operates in the wild in pairs or small families, is extremely fond of fruits.

blue tinge, the majority of the tail (upper side) being dark-green. The wing feathers are blackish with whitish to straw-yellow edges. The shoulders and head also have feathers of this color arrangement, giving a scalloped appearance. A large, black shoulder patch is typical of this variety, giving further accentuation to the scalloping of head and shoulders.

The yellow head and red bridle and forehead band are also typical. The eyes are brown, the beak is grayish-yellow, and the feet are gray-brown. According to Karl Neunzig, the hen is smaller than the cock, but I have found this not always to be the case. A somewhat better method of sex determination is to measure the head, which is markedly larger in the cock than in the hen. However, the breeding season will soon tell us if we have a true pair!

Size: 12½ to 14⅛ inches (32–36 cm): tail, 6⅓ to 6¾ inches (16–17 cm). Weight: cock, 3¾ to 4¾ ounces (109–136 g); hen, 3¾ to 4 ounces (105–117 g). Leg band: ¹⁵⁄₆₄ inch (6 mm).

Juveniles are often difficult to distinguish from the adults as they obtain adult plumage within 12 months; from fledging to one year old, the yellow color is duller.

Like the Adelaide rosella, this variety inhabits the bush land of southeastern South Australia and some border regions of New South Wales and Victoria. They are especially attracted to areas with adequate water and they frequently are seen along rivers, such as the Murray and Murrumbidgee, often in groups of 10 to 12 pairs. The life-style is similar to that of the Adelaide rosella. It is unfortunate that this variety is not more readily available for our aviaries. In Australia, they frequently are kept and are recognized as good captive breeders. The bird also has been bred in other countries. The hen lays four to six eggs, but in the wild may lay up to eight, about $^{15}\!/_{16}$ by $^{25}\!/_{32}$ inch (24 x 20 mm). At first it was thought that the birds would not breed in captivity under any circumstances, but success has been achieved in recent years.

It seems that the yellow rosella was first imported into Denmark; the literature tells us that young specimens were reared successfully in Copenhagen in 1892. Breeding results are reported from England in 1904. According to Dr. Groen, the variety was exhibited in the London Zoo already in 1897. It is impossible to estimate when the first specimens arrived in Europe, but the above tells us they obviously have been known to European aviculture for many years.

If you are fortunate enough to obtain a pair of these delightful birds, your first concern will be to ensure that they are properly acclimatized (i.e. contraband birds from Australia, or European bred birds). As soon as the birds are acclimatized and accustomed to their new (not too small) aviary, they may be given nesting facilities in the form of a large box or hollow log containing a bed of peat-dust or sawdust.

The birds do not exactly have what could be called a pretty song, but their calls are not so nerve racking as those of some parrot species.

In addition to the normal parakeet food, they should receive a choice of green foods; this being particularly important during the breeding season. Additional seeds, such as those of lettuce, poppy, and various weeds, as well as ant pupae and mealworms, also may be given. In order to have a better chance of successful breeding, each variety (and pair) of rosellas should be kept in separate aviaries. They are very quarrelsome among each other and with other parrot-like birds, especially in the breeding season. Small, finch-like birds can, however, be kept together with rosellas without any danger to them, even when they are nesting.

The incubation period for the yellow rosella, like other rosella varieties, is 18 days.

Yellow-bellied Rosella— *Platycercus caledonicus*

caledonicus: from (New) Caledonia. This is an error as the species does not occur there.

Platycercus caledonicus. When alighting, the green rosella—the largest representative of the rosella group— has a habit of spreading its long, broad tail. The nest box should be placed in a somewhat cool position in the aviary; the young cannot tolerate high temperatures.

The Species

Description: Both sexes are greenish-yellow colored on the underside. The throat is blue; the forehead is red. The edges of the wings are blue as is the underside of the tail feathers. The mantle feathers are deep black, edged with green. Juvenile specimens are mainly greenish in color and thus easy to distinguish from adults. It is difficult to distinguish the sexes, but the hen is somewhat duller and paler in color than the cock; the yellow color in particular is usually paler in the hen. The red color on the forehead is also paler in the hen and somewhat narrower. There is also a difference in the size of the beak and the head, those of the hen being markedly smaller. The young lose their juvenile plumage at the second molt—between thirteen and sixteen months of age—and take on the colors of the adults. In most cases, the size of head and beak alone is enough to distinguish the sexes.

Size: 12½ to 14⅛ inches (32–36 cm) including a 6¾-inch (17-cm) long tail. Weight: cock, 3¾ to 5⅝ ounces (105–165 g); hen, 3⅛ to 4½ ounces (90–130 g). Leg band: ¹⁵⁄₆₄ inch (6 mm).

Voice: The alarm call is loud, high, and piercing; on sensing danger this call is repeated twice by each bird. The contact call consists of two or three bell-like tones. A group of several birds feeding on the ground have a different, flute-like call, which also is probably a form of contact call. This latter call is often heard also as the birds settle for the night. Birds resting or sunning themselves during the day will let out a continuous chattering and twittering among themselves. The birds are very strongly bound to their habitat.

Nest: In a hollow trunk or limb, usually a eucalyptus. The hen lays four to five, occasionally six, eggs. These are cream-colored and almost round about 1.2 by ¹⁵⁄₁₆ inch (30 x 24 mm). Outside the breeding season, adults form groups of five to ten, whereas juvenile birds will gather in groups of 20 or more.

Distribution: Found in Tasmania and the islands of the Bass Strait. The birds can cause much damage in tree plantations and orchards and frequently are culled in great numbers. In Tasmania the "common" rosella (*P. eximius*), unlike the yellow-bellied rosella, is fully protected. In the wild, the yellow-bellied rosella may be seen in some color variations. Those that live in the west coast rainforests are greener, whereas those from the drier east coast are yellower in color.

Remarks: These birds are fairly easy to breed in captivity and two breeds per season is not unusual. It is best to keep each pair separately in its own aviary. The nest box 23⅔ inches (60 cm) high with inside measurements of 7.9 by 7.9 inches (20 cm x 20 cm); entrance hole, 3.2 to 3.5 inches (8–9 cm) can be given in April and hung in the flight. A layer of peat mulch or sawdust should be placed in the box.

It is interesting to note that the hen rosella may spend quite a long time in the nest box before the first egg is laid. In the wild, I have observed several times that the hen spends two or three weeks in the nest before laying eggs. During this time, the cock stays in the vicinity and often feeds the hen in the nest.

This variety is probably the hardiest of the rosellas and can withstand cold weather very well; it is also one of the most peaceful. The yellow-bellied rosella is probably the oldest and most primitive of the eight varieties. I find them most beautiful immediately after the molt. After a time, unfortunately, the plumage can look a bit tattered; in the wild, the greener form seems to have a bigger problem with this than the yellow one.

Mutations: None.

Stanley or Western Rosella— *Platycercus icterotis*

icterotis: yellow ear; *xanthogenys:* yellow cheek; Stanley: Edward Smith Stanley, thirteenth Duke of Derby (1775–1851), who amassed one of Europe's greatest animal collections, which included many species of birds.

The Species

Platycercus icterotis. In the quest for nesting sites, the quiet Stanely or western rosella—the smallest representative of the genus *Platycercus* —often suffers defeat in the wild against the more aggressive twenty-eight parakeet.

Description: This beautiful bird is prized by aviculturists as it makes an ideal aviary bird. The cock has a light red scalp, throat, breast, and belly, occasionally with a sprinkling of yellow feathers. The flanks are also frequently red, and with a yellowish tinge in the male. The cock's breast (especially in wild specimens) is frequently ornamented with glossy green patches. The throat and cheeks form a wide, yellow band, which in the cock reaches the eye but in the hen is narrower and paler. The cheek patch merges into white just below the gray-yellow beak. The back and rump are green with black "checks." The mantle feathers are deep black edged with green or sometimes reddish green. The flight feathers are strongly built so that, in the wild, the birds can develop a fast flight. The edges of the narrow wings are blue. The tail is greenish-blue on the upper side. The hen is somewhat smaller than the cock and also a little duller in color. The red and the blue (in the tail, for example) are nowhere near as deep and bright. Some captive bred examples frequently show large amounts of green in the red areas, the head sometimes being more green than red. In captive bred birds, the cocks and hens are frequently indistinguishable in color, though the hen remains somewhat smaller than the cock.

Size: 10¼ to 11 inches (26–28 cm); tail, 5⅛ to 6 inches (13–15 cm). Weight: cock, 2 to 2⅝ ounces (58–82 g); hen, 1⅝ to 2½ ounces (52–72 g). Leg band: about 7⁄32 inch (5.4 mm).

Voice: Soft, not unpleasant, flute-like chattering ("clink-clink").

Nest: In a hollow in a eucalyptus tree. The hen lays three to seven, but usually five white eggs; about 1 by ⅞ inch (26 x 22 mm). The hen broods the eggs for 19–20 days. The hen leaves the nest in the early morning and the late afternoon in order to be fed by the cock. He also feeds her in the nest after the young have hatched and helps feed the young.

Distribution: Occurs in the wetter parts of south west Australia where they inhabit open woodland, wooded margins of agricultural land, along waterways, and in plantations. This parakeet is common around human habitations where it is tolerated well.

Remarks: Fledglings are mainly green and resemble the hen at first. Experienced breeders are able to sex the young by looking at the forehead feathers; those of the hen are light colored, whereas cocks have dark, reddish brown feathers. In both sexes, the throat and cheek markings are not clear until after the first molt in August/September, sometimes in the beginning of October, when determination of sexes becomes much easier. The first molt occurs about three months after the young leave the nest, but the cocks do not have full adult plumage until one year old.

In the wild, these birds live in pairs or in groups of up to ten pairs when they can cause much damage to crops and plantations.

The Stanley is the only rosella found in its particular habitat. There are two well-documented subspecies. The first, *P. i. icterotis*, occurs along the coast and is redder in color and stronger in pattern, has a wider and more yellow cheek patch and a smaller body than the second, *P. i. xanthogenys*, which occurs inland and is recognizable by its narrow cheek patch and weaker color pattern.

The Stanley rosella is a fairly peaceful bird, but I would still recommend that each pair have a separate aviary in the breeding season so that good breeding results are enhanced. These rosellas also quickly become tame. In a quiet aviary, a pair will breed quickly. Any unused nest boxes should, of course, be removed from the aviary. The nest box (a horizontal box 23⅔ by 9.8 by 9.8 inches (60 x 15 x 25 cm) or a vertical box 19.5 inches (50 cm) high with a floor 7.9 by 7.9 inches (20 x 20 cm) should be provided with a layer of peat-dust or sawdust. It is also recommended that, in dry weather, the box is lightly sprayed with water from a garden hose, in order to increase humidity. In general, the birds produce a single brood each year, although wild birds produce up to three broods per annum. The young are sexually mature at twelve to sixteen months, although they may still carry juvenile plumage. Personally, I like to see my birds in full adult plumage before allowing them to breed; this will occur by eighteen months. The hen alone broods the eggs. As soon as the young hatch, the birds should be given soaked (stale) white bread with egg yolk, universal food and rearing food, germinated seed (especially mixed weed seeds), and ant pupae (a food, which outside the breeding season, usually is ignored). Of course the usual good commercial parakeet seed mix, a rich variety of green food, fruit, and fresh water must be available at all times. In order to ensure successful breeding, we should not inspect the nest too often. As the birds grow, we gradually can reduce the special food and increase the normal food: millet, sunflowerseed, cracked corn, canary grass seed, and hemp. The latter seed should be given only in small quantities, otherwise the birds will become too fat. The birds will take green food greedily and are especially fond of young lettuce, leaf buds, and germinated seeds. These birds can spend the winter in an outside aviary, provided they have a damp- and draft- proof night shelter; but as they are so valuable, I personally prefer to overwinter them in roomy, indoor aviaries if space permits; do not give a nest box in such a situation, otherwise unhealthy winter breeding may result.

Stanley rosellas have been isolated from other rosellas for so long that they have taken a fairly distant relationship. This is apparent in the smaller size, the sexual dimorphism, their hardiness, and the absence of cheek patches in the young. They are therefore regarded by some experts (Forshaw and Lendon, for example) to be a link between the genera *Platycercus* and *Psephotus* (red-rumps, and so on), especially as their method of flight resembles the latter.

Like other rosella species, Stanleys are fond of bathing. They are quite hardy in our climate but require a minimum of 10 feet (3 m) flying space. They are very suitable for the beginner.

It would be useful to try to keep the two subspecies separate and to breed pure races so that they can be propagated in the future.

Mutations: None.

Eastern Rosella—*Platycercus eximius*

eximius: excellent, outstanding; *cecilae:* after Cecilia, a family member of G. M. Mathews; *diemenensis:* from van Diemensland, former name of Tasmania.

Description: The breast, shoulders, neck, and head are light red. There is a white cheek patch. The back is yellow with greenish-black edges to the feathers. The rump is greenish-yellow. The primary wing feathers are blue and the tail is blue with white bands, the central tail feathers green; the underside of the tail base is red. The eyes are brown, the beak is grayish-white, the feet are blackish-brown. The red on the hen is not so bright and she has a smaller beak and grayish-white cheek patches. There is no

The Species

Platycercus eximius. The eastern rosella often is kept in cages as a pet. Once the bird loses its fear of humans, it often becomes rather aggressive. In the wild, the species occasionally raids cultivated crops and orchards.

definitive dimorphism other than the small, grayish-brown feathers around the eyes of the hen, which fail in the cock. Young birds are very green in the neck region.

Size: 11¾ inches (30 cm); tail, 6⅓ to 7 inches (16–18 cm). Weight: cock, 3⅜ to 4¼ ounces (96–121 g); hen, 3¼ ounces (90 g). Leg band: about ⁷⁄₃₂ inch (5.4 mm).

Voice: A loud "kwink-kwink," sometimes metallic. Birds surprised will let out a number of shrill screams. When feeding, the birds let out a continuous pleasant chatter.

Nest: In hollow limbs up to several yards (meters) from the ground. I have found nests in old tree stumps and even in fence posts. The hen lays four to nine, but usually five, white eggs, about 1 by ²⁹⁄₃₂ inch (27 x 23 mm).

Distribution: Found in plantations, gardens, wooded savannas, open woodland, in trees along water courses, around agricultural land, villages, even into the suburbs of larger towns and cities,

from southern Queensland through New South Wales into Victoria and the southeastern part of South Australia, extending to the west of Adelaide. The subspecies *P. e. diemenensis* with more intense red on the head, larger cheek patches and a light-blue rump, occurs in Tasmania. In southwestern Queensland and northeastern New South Wales south to the Hunter river, another subspecies, *P. e. cecilae*, occurs. This has a deeper red head and breast and the back and wing feathers are edged with yellow. The rump is bluish-green. Known as the golden-mantled rosella, this variety is discussed in greater detail below.

Remarks: Rosellas are known as good breeders although the cocks can sometimes become rather aggressive; the best results are obtained from birds in excess of twelve months of age. Before that, the birds have not sufficiently developed their adult plumage to easily distinguish the sexes. They require a nest box 19½ by 8 by 8 inches (50 cm high x 20 x 20 cm) and an entrance hole of 2⅓ inches (6 cm) diameter. The cock will feed the hen during brooding but will not brood himself! The birds will breed from mid-February to May. The young hatch after 18–20 days, sometimes a little longer, and are fed by the cock as well as the hen, although the male starts foraging for the young after about ten days. The young leave the nest at about 30 days and are in full adult plumage after 10–15 months. Mature birds must be separated and used for breeding when they are in full color. In the wild, these birds live in pairs or in large groups where they frequently forage for seeds, and so on, on open ground dotted with trees and scrub. Flowers, buds, nectar, fruit, and insects and their larvae are also eaten. In some

Top left and right: Red-vented blue bonnet and Naretha ▶ blue bonnet parakeets. The latter is the smallest representative of the blue bonnets—a somewhat inaccurate name as the face, not the bonnet or cap, is blue. Bottom: The red-fronted kakariki. Kakarikis differ from rosellas by the absence of the small notch on the upper mandible, and the overall bright green coloration of the back.

horticultural areas, the birds can cause severe damage to crops and plantations. The fluting call is not unpleasant to the ear. They are not in the least shy birds, either in the wild or in captivity; in Australia, I have found that one can approach them quite closely before they take flight. Many of these birds are killed in traffic.

The name rosella arose from the village of Rosehill, near Parramatta—a suburb of Sydney. As Cayley states: "The early days of settlement; the name Rosella (originally Rosehiller) is derived from Rosehill (named after the English settler George Rose)."

It is interesting to note that in northeast New South Wales and southeastern Queensland, this species frequently pairs with the blue-cheeked rosella. The birds have become acclimatized in New Zealand where they were imported by enthusiasts years ago.

In Holland, the first breeding successes occurred in 1885, and a good pair will produce year after year. In captivity, the birds can remain fertile for 25 to 30 years! However a cock may not be interested in any old hen placed with him and should be given a number of choices (not all at once of course!) until a suitable mate is found. A hen that does not suit a cock's fancy will be pursued aggressively and must be removed immediately. Once a compatible pair has been found, you will have few further problems. A good means of producing a wider choice of cocks and hens is to cooperate with your fellow breeders.

Mutations: At the present time, there are five well-documented mutations: lutino, white-wing, pastel, isabel, and red. The lutino appeared some years ago in Australia, but since seems to have

disappeared. The white-wing was first bred in Belgium; it has a yellow tail, light-colored feet, a golden-yellow back with hardly any black; the head is more yellow than red and there is a yellow stripe above the eye. It is genetically dominant.

The isabel and the pastel are very similar. The isabel is more brown tinted, especially in the wing feathers. In the pastel, this brown leans more towards gray. The isabel is genetically sex-linked recessive, the pastel is autosomal recessive.

The red rosella is especially beautiful. The whole of the belly and breast are a uniform red, whereas red feathers also occur on the back. The belly feathers have a white background, which can be seen easily if the feathers are blown. The tail of the hen is lighter than that of the cock. Both sexes have a white stripe on the underside of the wing, but that of the hen is wider. This variety is, in fact, an opaline mutation that is genetically sex-linked recessive.

The Golden-mantled Rosella—
Platycercus eximius cecilae

Already mentioned above, this subspecies has a length of 11.8 to 12.6 inches (30–32 cm); the wings are 6 to 6.7 inches (15–17 cm) long and the tail is 6.3 to 7 inches (16–18 cm). It is unfortunate that this variety is not so readily available in the trade as it is indeed an ideal aviary bird always ready to breed given the right conditions. They become very tame and will even learn to feed from the hand quite quickly. These birds also offer possibilities to the enthusiast with a small purse. I have seen one-year-old birds breed well and two broods per year is no exception. They also make excellent foster parents, even for other (more expensive) rosella species. They also can be crossed with other rosellas, but the young are not so pretty as the originals and it will require much patience and many generations to reproduce the pure subspecific patterns and colors. These birds require a roomy aviary, and can be kept peacefully with other small finches and so on, but a pair should not be kept with other parrotlike birds as "war" will soon develop.

◄ A pair of Australian king parakeets. These colorful birds like large branches in the aviary. The sexes are noticeably different in some of their calls and in their magnificent colors. It takes the male approximately two and half years to attain full adult plumage.

The Species

Platycercus eximius cecilae. The golden-mantled rosella, although originally a native of northeast Australia and Tasmania, is now well established in the vicinity of Auckland and near Dunedin, New Zealand.

The eastern rosella makes a good example of Gloger's Law; the golden-mantled rosella occurs in dry areas, the nominate form in wet areas.

Blue-cheeked Rosella—*Platycercus adscitus*

adscitus: adopted, new; *palliceps:* pale-headed

Description: Both sexes are similar in color. The main colors are yellow and blue. The head is yellowish-white with white cheeks; the breast and belly are sky-blue, as are the wing coverts and the tail; the underside of the tail is light red. The primaries are dark, with red highlights. The tail tip is white and the whole tail is banded with green; the under tail coverts are red. The rump is greenish-yellow; the back is yellow with black "check" marking. The eyes are dark brown, the beak is grayish-yellow, and the feet are dark gray.

Size: 11¾ to 13 inches (30–33 cm); tail, 6 to 6¾ inches (154–17 cm). Weight: cock and hen, 4½ to 4¾ ounces (129–132 g). Leg band: ¹⁵⁄₆₄ inch (6 mm).

Voice: Same as "common" rosella.

Nest: In a hollow limb (usually a eucalyptus or similar tree). The hen lays three to seven white eggs, about 1 by ⅞ inch (27 x 22 mm), which are brooded for about 20 days. The young leave the nest at about five weeks of age.

Distribution: Found in northeastern Australia. Introduced into Hawaii in 1877, but wild living specimens not seen since the 1930s. There are two recognized subspecies: *P. a. adscitus*, found on Cape York Peninsula and south to the Mitchell River and Cairns, and *P. a. palliceps* (pale-headed or mealy rosella) found from Cairns south to northern New South Wales. This latter subspecies is very common in aviculture.

Remarks: The bird is a "tough cookie," and is bred both in Europe and the United States. Once acclimatized, the bird may be kept outside all year provided it has a draft- and rain-proof shelter and a

Platycercus adscitus. Generally similar in color to the adult male, the adult hen of the blue-cheeked rosella sometimes has a pale underwing stripe, which is normally absent in her partner.

112

The Species

Platycercus palliceps. The pale-headed or mealy rosella differs from the nominate form especially in having white cheek patches and a white head, tinged with yellow.

choice of sleeping boxes. In such cases however, males and females should be separated to prevent out of season breeding. In the breeding season, each pair should be provided with a separate aviary. Breeding "overtures" may start as early as late January for these lively and frequently aggressive birds. You should take care to select only healthy and fully acclimatized birds for early breeding. Birds kept in aviaries with outdoor flights are usually keener to breed than those kept indoors. The nesting box (floor area 9.8 by 9.8 inches (25 x 25 cm); height, 13¾ inches (35 cm); entrance hole, 3.5 inches (9 cm) in diameter), should be provided with a layer of wood shavings, pulp, or peat. The hen (usually) will then gnaw and arrange it to her liking and throw any excess material out of the box. The box should be placed preferably in the open part of the aviary so that it receives some rain and keeps the necessary humidity up. In long periods of dry weather, you should mist spray the nest box

daily, preferably in the evening. Another method of maintaining humidity is to have a false bottom in the nest-box, below the brood hollow (in which a few holes are bored). A shallow dish of water placed below will ensure adequate moisture for the developing eggs. The birds like to bathe and must have good facilities to do so, especially in the breeding season.

Two broods per year are not unusual. It is interesting to note that, unlike most rosella species, the young of this species soon become tame and will readily accept tidbits from the fingers. The young develop their adult plumage at about sixteen months of age, and may be used for breeding at the end of their second year.

Mutations: There exists a very rare pastel mutation that is somewhat lighter than the normal wild color.

Brown's Rosella—*Platycercus venustus*

venustus: after Venus, the Roman goddess of love.

Description: As it is so difficult to distinguish the sexes, one should obtain some kind of a written guarantee from the dealer when purchasing birds, to ensure that you can exchange birds if they do not turn out to be true pairs. Sexually mature birds sometimes can be distinguished in that the hen has a grayish-black head as compared to the deep black head of the cock. But, in my experience, this difference is not always present. Once I had a pair that were virtually indistinguishable; frequently one must leave it to sheer luck that one has a pair.

The normal bird has a deep brownish-black to deep black scalp and back of the head. The cheeks are white, the throat is light blue. There is frequently a red fleck on the forehead. The back and the wing feathers are black with broad, yellow edges, giving the appearance of an attractive checkered pattern. The larger wing coverts are light blue with purple overtones. The primaries are dark brown, frequently

The Species

Platycercus venustus. In the wild, Brown's rosella unfortunately is declining rapidly in numbers, the cause of which is unknown. The species operates in pairs or family groups near tall forests, and likes spending many hours high in the trees.

light green at the tips. The tail is partly bluish-green with the larger feathers black banded and spotted with white. The lower belly feathers are red, as are the feathers under the tail base. The eyes are blackish-brown, the beak is light gray frequently with a blue tip; the feet are dark brown.

Size: 11 to 11½ inches (28–29 cm); tail, 5½ to 6 inches (14–15 cm). Weight: cock, 3¼ to 4 ounces (92–112 g); hen, 3⅛ to 3¼ ounces (88–92 g). Leg band: about 7⁄32 inch (5.4 mm).

Voice: A somewhat metallic two-toned call ("clink-clink"), which is repeated several times. When foraging in the tree tops, one can hear a slow continual chattering ("kwink-kwink" or "pee-pit-tee").

Nest: In hollow limbs or trunks. The hen lays two to four, sometimes five white eggs, about 1 by

53⁄64 inch (26 x 21 mm). These hatch in about 20 days.

Distribution: Found in open woodland, especially along water courses, in the northwestern and northern parts of Australia from the Kimberleys, across the Northern Territory and touching into Queensland; also on the islands of Bathurst, Melville, and Milingimbi.

Remarks: These rosellas are naturally quiet and peaceful and in the wild live in flocks of 8 to 15 pairs. When not foraging on the ground, they like to spend time in the treetops. During the breeding season (in Australia from June to late August), the pairs split up on their own to nest. The birds are named after Robert Brown, who first described them in 1820; according to some ornithologists, he was the first to discover the species. In captivity, Brown's rosella is quite difficult to breed as it tends to molt in our summer and get ready to breed in October, sometimes even later. The cold weather causes frequent cases of egg binding. The birds should be given ample supplies of clean green food, and a good make of breeding and rearing food. In the wild, breeding birds take many beetles, caterpillars and other insects. Breeding birds should be at least a year old. I have noticed several times that a cock which has had another hen will seldom settle happily or even accept a new partner. In the wild, as my wife has discovered, the birds pair for life. If we have a compatible true pair, we can expect some breeding results, though I would recommend that winter breeding be avoided if at all possible. Summer breeding also has its problems. Once a hen has made a choice of nest box (height, 21⅔ inches (55 cm); floor area, 7.9 by 7.9 inches (20 x 20 cm), entrance hole, 2⅓ inches (6 cm) diameter), other boxes should be removed or she may lay eggs in more than one box and a breeding failure will result. The flight should be at least 13 to 16 feet (4–5 m) long. We should try to get the birds to breed in the months from May to July for the best results. Moist sawdust and/or peat-dust should be laid on the floor of the nest box. Young birds are fed with green food,

114

(fresh twigs also may be given) ant "eggs," and mealworms, as well as the normal parakeet seed mixture. The hen broods on her own and leaves the nest five or six times per day to be fed by the cock. The cock also helps in raising the young, which leave the nest in about 35 days but are still cared for by the adults for a further three weeks or so. As soon as the young are reasonably independent and can feed themselves, they should be removed from the aviary before fighting occurs. If there is time left for another brood, the hen should again be given a choice of nest boxes. Although these birds were first imported into England at the beginning of the century, successful breeding did not occur until 1928 (by the Duke of Bedford). But we have to thank the English breeder Holmes Watkins for the fact that these birds are still legally available today outside Australia. Breeding in Holland and Belgium, for example, took place after the second world war.

Brown's rosella does not easily adjust to the climates and seasonal changes of eastern and middle America, or of the greater part of Europe. This means that the birds frequently come into breeding condition at the end of the summer and breed in the fall. It will be necessary to provide additional care and to supply supplementary lighting as the days shorten, and perhaps heating in the shelter. The young will cool and die much quicker in a cold, damp fall than they would in Australia's tropical north.

Brown's rosella is therefore not an easy bird to breed and is really only suitable for experienced fanciers. The biggest problem is in acquiring a true and compatible pair; they are very particular in their choice of partner. Cock birds also can be very aggressive and have been known to kill an unsuitable partner. The fancier must therefore keep a continual eye on his birds. They require a large aviary and should be minimally disturbed during breeding.

Mutations: None.

Barnard's or Mallee Ringneck Parakeet—*Barnardius barnardi*

Barnardi: Edward Barnard (1786–1861) was an important civil servant in the British Crown Colonies and he had a deep interest in plants and animals; *Mallee:* several species of low growing shrubby eucalyptus that thrive in the drier parts of the Australian bush. There is no main trunk but a number of trunklets emerging from the ground. Barnard's parakeets inhabit the mallee areas in Australia; *whitei:* Samuel Albert White (1870–1954) was born in Adelaide (South Australia) and undertook several expeditions into the Australian outback in search of birds; *macgillivrayi:* Alexander Sykes Macgillivray (1853–1907) was an Australian farmer and amateur ornithologist who discovered the Cloncurry parakeet; *Cloncurry:* A town in Queensland, Australia, in the area in which the Cloncurry parakeet occurs.

Barnardius barnardi. The rather tempermental Bernard's or mallee ringneck parakeet needs a large aviary. The species also prefers a grandfather clock nest box, which should be placed on the aviary floor.

The Species

Description: The yellow neck ring is seen on all *Barnardius* species. The areas around the beak and behind the eyes are blue. The forehead has a red band; the neck, back, and secondary wing feathers are blue. The wings are green and yellow, the primaries and tail feathers are blue, and the shoulders are yellow. The hen may be distinguished from the cock by her dark gray-green back and nape. The eyes are dark brown, the beak is pale gray, and the feet are gray. Young birds resemble the adult hen, but the crown is mainly brown in color. They reach full color in 12 to 18 months and the males lose the wing stripe.

Size: 13¾ inches (35 cm) including the 7-inch (17.5-cm) tail. Weight: cock, 3⅝ to 5 ounces (110–143 g); hen, 3⅔ to 4⅝ ounces (104–138 g). Leg band: ¹⁵⁄₆₄ inch (6 mm).

Voice: A loud trilling, frequently repeated "kwink, kwink." Alarm call is a coarse, penetrating, and metallic "chuk, chuk, chuk." Foraging birds chatter and chuckle continuously to one another.

Nest: In hollow limbs or trunks, especially in the mallee types of eucalyptus. The nest hollow is lined with wood pulp. The hen lays four to six, but usually five white, roundish, about 1 by ²⁹⁄₃₂ inch (29 x 23 mm), eggs and these are brooded by her alone for about 20 days. After a further 30 days, the young leave the nest but they require further parental care for some time longer.

Distribution: Found inland of eastern Australia (east of 138 degrees). The subspecies *B. b. barnardi* occurs in the southeast, but not in the area of the somewhat smaller *B. b. whitei*, which is found in the Flinders Ranges (South Australia). This subspecies is a duller green, while the nape and back are gray-green, sometimes dark green, and the head is brownish. The *B. b. macgillivrayi* (the Cloncurry parakeet) is found in northeastern Queensland. This subspecies lacks the red band on the forehead and is altogether greener in color. In Australia, this is an especially popular aviary bird.

Remarks: In the wild, these birds live together in pairs or small groups. They eat the seeds of

Barnardius macgillivrayi. The most noticeable difference between the Cloncurry parakeet (pictured) and the mallee ringneck (page 115) is the lack of the red frontal band above the beak.

grasses and other plants, fruit, flowers, buds and shoots, insects and their eggs and larvae. During the heat of the day they like to hide themselves in shady foliage, becoming active again towards the evening. The brooding hen leaves the nest to feed only in the early morning and late afternoon while her mate stays near to the nest and warns her of any possible danger. In captivity the birds require a roomy aviary for each pair as they can be very agressive; they should be given a daily supply of fresh twigs. They require similar care to other rosellas previously described. They should be left in peace once they start breeding. Nest box: 24 by 8 by 8 inches (60 x 20 x 20 cm) with an entrance hole 2⅓ inches (6 cm) in diameter.

Mutations: There is an autosomal recessive blue mutation in which all yellow color is missing, being replaced by white.

The Species

Port Lincoln Parakeet—
Barnardius zonarius

Port Lincoln: A South Australian port; *zonarius:* with a band or ring; *semitorquatus:* half-collared; *occidentalis:* westerly.

Barnardius zonarius. The very adaptable Port Lincoln parakeet is primarily a ground dweller. It has an undulated flight, and in the wild as well as in captivity is very active, even after sunset and on moonlit nights.

Description: Cock and hen are very similar in color. The head is black, the cheeks and throat are blue. There is a yellow band across the throat, whereas the breast and the back are grass-green. The belly is yellowish with green overtones. The wings are green with blue primaries and the tail is dark green with blue on top and blue outer feathers. Sometimes the hen has a slightly browner head. The young also have a brown head and wing stripes. The eyes are brown, the beak is light gray, and the feet are gray.

Size: 15 inches (37.5 cm) including the 7½-inch (19-cm) long tail. Weight: cock, 5 to 6 ounces (142–170 g); hen, 4.2 to 4.8 ounces (120–136 g). Leg band: ¹⁵⁄₆₄ inch (6 mm).

Voice: A high, clear and quickly repeated whistle; the alarm call is metallic and similar to that of the Barnard's parakeet.

Nest: In a hollow eucalyptus limb. The hen lays four to seven, but usually five white and roundish eggs, about 1.2 by 1 inch (31 x 25 mm). The base of the nest is lined with wood pulp.

Distribution: Found in central and western Australia. *B. z. zonarius* is the best known subspecies. *B. z. semitorquatus,* the so-called twenty eight parakeet (as its call is said to resemble the words "twenty-eight") is a little larger and has a red forehead band. It is found only in southwestern Australia (south of Perth and west of Albany). *B. z. occidentalis* is also found in Western australia and is paler in color and somewhat smaller.

Remarks: This is a noisy bird both in the wild and in the aviary. It forages mainly on the ground for food, but also among the twigs of trees and shrubs. They usually stay in single pairs or small (family) groups, but can still be a pest to agriculture. In order to breed successfully, each pair requires a roomy aviary. Young birds develop adult plumage

Barnardius semitorquatus. The hardy and friendly twenty-eight parakeet is the largest representative of the broad-tailed parakeets, and makes a good pet if obtained young; it even learns to whistle. It should be housed in an aviary, never in a cage.

The Species

at seventeen to eighteen months, and are sexually mature at two years.

Nesting behavior is similar to that of the Barnard's parakeet. In the wild, the nest site is chosen by the hen and is often in higher eucalyptus along water courses. The nest entrance may be 10 to 50 feet (3–5 m) above the ground and the diameter of the whole is often not more than 8 inches (20 cm). In the aviary, a nest box 24 to 28 inches (60–70 cm) high and with a floor area of 8 by 8 inches (20 x 20 cm) is ideal. The entrance hole should be 3 inches (7.5 cm) in diameter.

In the aviary, the birds can be encouraged to breed in March so the nest box should be installed early in the year. I personally experienced birds that started to breed as early as January. The eggs are brooded for about 20 days and the young are fed by the hen only until they are ten to fourteen days old, then by both parents. They fledge at about five weeks, but in the wild they will stay with their parents for several months. In the aviary, Port Lincoln parakeets will spend a lot of time on the floor. They will appreciate fresh twigs to gnaw at. As they are good fliers, the aviary should be at least 17 feet (5 m) long. They are hardy birds, that with good care, will live for ten to eighteen years.

Mutations: None. The twenty eight parakeet has an autosomal recessive blue mutation, but this is very scarce. It is interesting to note that this subspecies spends more time in the trees than does the Port Lincoln. The twenty eight parakeet is found in the wettest part of the *Barnardius* range. Trees grow to 264 feet (80 m) and the birds nest high up in them. In the aviary, a similar sized nest box as described for the Port Lincoln should be placed as high up as possible, and the entrance hole should be 3 inches (8 cm) in diameter. The twenty eight parakeet is not easy to breed and it is an agressive bird, requiring a spacious aviary. It is a renowned gnawer of woodwork, and aviaries should thus be strengthened with metal as a precaution. Even thin mesh is seldom spared, and quickly bitten to pieces!

Red-rumped Parakeet—*Psephotus haematonotus*

Psephotus: with mosaic pattern; *haematonotus:* blood (and) back; *caeruleus:* dark blue.

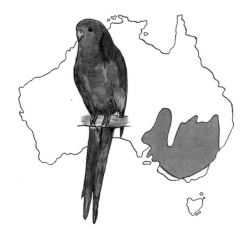

Psephotus haematonotus. Competing with starlings and sparrows for proper nest sites, many red-rumped parakeets use nest boxes provided by concerned individuals. This hardy species is almost the ideal aviary bird—always ready to breed, a caring foster parent, intelligent, long lived, and very pretty!

Description: The cock is mainly green with a yellow underside (with orange undertones). The back is light red with yellow undertones. The under tail coverts are white, sometimes with a little green. The wings are mainly blue and the shoulders are yellow. The upper tail coverts are green and the central tail feathers are green with blue undertones. Outer tail feathers are blue with lighter edges. The eyes are brown, the beak is black, and the feet are gray. The hen is mainly olive-greenish-brown with a little orange in the neck and belly. It has a pale blue shoulder patch and a gray beak. The young are, at first, similar to the hen, but the young females already have a pale beak.

The Species

Size: 10⅔ inches (27 cm) including the 5½-inch (14-cm) long tail. Weight: cock, 2⅜ to 2½ ounces (68–70 g); hen, 2 to 2⅓ ounces (54–65 g). Leg band: ¹³⁄₆₄ inch (5 mm).

Voice: A two noted whistle. A soft, not unpleasant chattering and a louder chatter when tussling.

Nest: In a tree hollow, preferably close to water. The hen lays four to seven but usually five, white, roundish eggs, about ¹⁵⁄₆₄ by ¾ inch (24 x 19 mm). These are brooded by the hen alone for about 20 days. The hen broods very closely (also in the wild) and will sit even in the face of real danger; I have personally tried to push a hen from her clutch several times, but she will sit tightly and not even panic! At about thirty days of age, the young leave the nest but are dependent on their parents for some time thereafter. The young are sexually mature at twelve months of age. Two, sometimes three, broods may be reared in a season.

Distribution: Found in southeastern Australia. The bird is quite common but scarcer in Victoria. It inhabits mainly grassland and agricultural areas. The subspecies *P. h. haematonotus* is replaced by *P. h. caeruleus* in South Australia (around Innamincka) in the Flinders Ranges, but it is not known if the races interbreed in the wild.

Remarks: These well-known and loved aviary birds like to forage on the ground both in the wild and in the aviary. For successful breeding a roomy nest box—13¾ inches (35 cm) high by 4¾ by 9.8 inches (12 x 25 cm); entrance hole 2⅓ inches (6 cm) in diameter—is necessary. As soon as they are feeding independently, the young should be separated from the parents as the cock can behave aggressively towards them, sometimes with dire results. Although this species behaves peaceably towards most other bird species, a pair should be kept away from others of their own kind or even other psittacines. I personally prefer to give each pair of red rumps a large aviary (at least 13 feet (4 m) long) to themselves. General care is similar to that required by the rosellas. Red-rumped parakeets are ideal birds for beginners to aviculture.

They may be used as foster parents, sometimes even for non-Australian parakeets! The foster youngsters must not, however, grow too large; but with smaller or similar sized species one usually can expect a successful outcome.

Mutations: In Australia several mutations are known, including lutino, cinnamon, fallow, blue, and pastel-blue. Unfortunately many of these are still not available in the United States or Europe.

The best-known mutation, which is generally available, is the yellow red-rumped parakeet. I am not too impressed with the chosen name as we are really talking about a cinnamon-mutation! Another not uncommon mutation is the olive (pied) red-rumped parakeet in which the red rump of the male is lost.

The "white" red-rumped parakeet, a product of yellow (cinnamon) x (pastel) blue is also gaining popularity. The white is really more silver, but in time, this will be improved. The mutation can only be produced via split-offspring.

In addition, there is the yellow mutation with red eyes. This is not silver-yellow as in the lutino, but more pastel colored. Fallow and cinammon are genetically sex-linked recessive, whereas the (pastel) blue, the lutino, and the olive (pied) are autosomal recessive.

Many-colored Parakeet— *Psephotus varius*

varius: many colored; *chrysopterygius:* golden-winged; *dissimilis:* dissimilar.

Description: It has a green breast and belly, lighter to blue on the head. The lower belly is red with yellowish highlights. There is a yellow forehead band, under tail coverts, and a conspicuous yellow shoulder patch often with orange highlights. The tail is green with two horizontal bands, one of which is light green, the other is deep red. The wing primaries and tail are blue. The hen is browner with light green under tail coverts. The

119

The Species

Psephotus varius. The many-colored parakeet, with its brilliant greens, purple, reds, and blues, lives in the wild in pairs or small family parties, especially inland. Rarely is it seen in coastal districts. It spends a large part of the day feeding on the ground.

shoulder patch is bright red; the forehead band is hardly discernible. The young are similar to the hen, but young cocks already show the red coloring, although faintly. Adult coloration is achieved in as little as six months.

Size: 10¼ inches (26 cm), including the 5½-inch (14-cm) long tail. Weight: cock, 1.9 to 2.3 ounces (55–66 g); hen, 2 to 2½ ounces (52–70 g). Leg band: ¹³⁄₆₄ inch (5 mm).

Voice: A number of fluting and pleasant tinkling tones.

Nest: In hollow limbs or trunks, usually 7 to 10 feet (2–3 m) from the ground. The hen lays four to six, but usually five white and roundish ⁶³⁄₆₄ by ¾ inch (25 x 19 mm) eggs. These are brooded by the hen alone for about 21 days. Both parents feed the nestlings, which leave the nest in about five weeks; parental care continues for a few more weeks.

Distribution: Found in central Australia, from southwestern Queensland to the middle of New South Wales and to northwest Victoria, central South Australia, and deep into Western Australia.

Remarks: In the wild, they occur in pairs or small (family) groups; however, where food is plentiful, they may congregate in large troops. They prefer low rainfall regions and are therefore nomadic in behavior, moving over large areas. They feed mainly on seeds, charcoal (the significance of which is not yet wholly understood; but perhaps it helps keep the nest dry in the breeding season), fruits, berries, and so on; they forage mainly on the ground. In the aviary, these are exceedingly charming birds, which, once acclimatized, are hardy and peaceful. However, the cock bird may become aggressive towards his male offspring if left too long after independence. It is recommended that pairs be kept singly in a large 13-foot (4 m) aviary as they can be aggressive towards other bird species. They may be fed on canary grass seed, sunflower seed, and a mixture of millets. A little hemp and a variety of green food, young shoots and buds, soaked corn, oats, plain cake, and milk-soaked, stale, white bread; berries, fruit, grass and weed seeds, charcoal, cuttlefish bone, and grit. Charcoal is important and one also can give burnt chicken bones. Pairs remain true to one another and will breed in a hollow log or nest box—17¾ inches (45 cm) high by 6 by 6 inches (15 x 15 cm); entrance hole, 2⅓ inches (6 mm) in diameter—provided they are left alone and in peace.

Mutations: None.

Hooded parakeet—*Psephotus chrysopterygius dissimilis*

This much prized parakeet from the Northern Territory requires similar care. The cock has a black cap and bluish-gray cheeks. The back and wings are brownish-black. The underside is greenish-blue to bluish-gray, the under tail coverts are pink. The tail is green, merging into black beneath. The tail has light blue edges and feathers. The central feathers

120

The Species

Psephotus chrysopterygius dissimilis. The hooded parakeet was first described in 1898 from a specimen obtained near the Mary River during the dry season as possessing a "singular jarring cry."

are brownish black; the main part of the body is deep yellow. The primary wing feathers are brownish-black. The beak is gray, the eyes are dark brown, and the feet are flesh colored. The hen is light green with a light blue underside and rump; the yellow in the wings is missing. Young males have no black on the head. The young reach full adult coloration at twelve to sixteen months.

This species, which is 10¼ inches (26 cm) long including the tail; weight: male, 1¾ to 2⅛ ounces (50–60 g); female, 2 to 2⅛ ounces (54–59 g); leg band: ¹³⁄₆₄ inch (5 mm), was first discovered by Professor K. Dahl in Arnhem Land in 1894. They live in pairs or in small groups in lightly wooded country but especially where an Australian grass species *(Triodia irritans)* occurs. Although they breed mainly in termite mounds in the wild, they will adapt to a nest box fairly readily in the aviary. The birds seem to want to breed in the middle of

winter! The prominent Dutch aviculturist R. R. P. van der Mark tells me in a letter: "Some pairs breed in our spring, as has happened by Dr. Y. Polak in Amersfoort and by the well-known breeder E. Boosey in England. Breeding successes have also occurred in Germany. Red-rump parakeets can be used as foster parents. Crossings with the yellow-shouldered parakeet, the red-rumped parakeet, the many colored parakeet and, at one time also, the paradise parakeet are possible! Unfortunately, there were in Europe in 1965 just 20 related breeding pairs and a few odd birds available. In 1962, Dr. R. Burkard of Zurich, Switzerland purchased a pair of hooded parakeets. These birds were about five years old and in excellent condition in spite of having been kept in a drafty old cage just 2 feet (60 cm) in length! The pair were a great worry for some time, but in the autumn of 1964, they showed the first signs of wanting to breed. Four youngsters eventually hatched but they starved to death through inadequate feeding. In December 1964, the pair began with a second brood; two young eventually hatched, apparently from the first and last egg, going by the difference in size. These left the nest in just ten days! Fortunately the hen continued to feed them. After the breeding pair had fully molted during the spring and summer, they bred again in August 1965, producing four young from four eggs. In October, the second brood produced three young from three eggs and in spite of already good breeding results the cock began again to court the hen after the last of the three had left the nest. This resulted in a further five eggs and five young, all of which left the nest in January and grew into fine, strong, young birds!"

Of the three different nest boxes offered—namely a rosella nest box, a 15¾ inch (40 cm) upright nest box, and a lovebird nest box fixed horizontally—the last was chosen although this seemed rather small for five young hooded parakeets! A mixture of wood shavings and peat was placed in a 1-inch (2-cm) deep layer on the floor of the box. The incubation period was 18 to 19 days and the young left the nest in about four weeks. At first they had difficulty in flying and landing properly on the perches, so Dr. Burkard lined the walls of the aviary with conifer tree branches. Although the young were fed by the parents for a further two weeks, they also helped themselves to food from the first day. The young resemble the hen in outward appearance, but the red color of the tail underside is not so bright and the beak is yellow and not horn colored.

Dr. Burkard's breeding pair was housed in his Exotic Finch House where they have a 10-foot (3-m) square indoor *and* outdoor flight. The indoor flight is warmed to 64° F (18° C) in the winter but 50 to 53.6° F (10–12° C) should be adequate to breed these birds. An automatic time switch is used to control photoperiod and switches on at 4:30 A.M.

Outside the breeding season, the hooded parakeets are supplied with various millets, spray millet, a few sunflower seeds, and green food. In the breeding season, they get soft food, germinated sunflower seeds, especially the striped and medium white; they are especially fond of green grass seed heads.

Let me add a few personal comments to the foregoing text. At about four months, the juvenile molt takes place and sometimes shows a faint sexual dimorphism. As the young cocks age, they may be recognized through their behavior; they are quickly excited, argue more, stand bolt upright and shake the tail back and forth. Between twelve to sixteen months the adult coloration is formed. We know that these birds are usually sexually mature in their second year, although occasional results have occurred at one year old.

Hooded parakeets are specialized in eating small grass seeds, which they take up from the ground or from the seed heads. They also eat a good amount of insects and green food. In the aviary they must have a variety of small seeds, and in the breeding season—especially after the young have hatched—they must have a supply of soaked germinated seed as well as various small insects.

Hooded parakeets breed in a similar manner to golden-shouldered parakeets (see page 00), that is in a tunnel excavated into a termite mound. I therefore use the same manner described for these birds in my hooded parakeet aviaries. I have discovered that these birds find it difficult to acclimatize to our eastern and middle American climates. They start to breed in September; the young are born in a cold period and various problems can ensue, especially when the hen leaves the newly hatched young alone in the nest for protracted periods (thus unwarmed). The later in the winter that breeding takes place, the greater the risks. An adequate heating system is thus essential. Although the hen may spend a lot of time in the nest during the first week, this does not mean that the young are necessarily warm enough. As soon as the young are thirty days old, one must keep a close eye on the male parent as he may attack his sons. It is thus best to remove the young from the aviary when they are four weeks old. We have learned from experience that hooded parakeets are more likely to breed if we keep several pairs in the same manner as we do the golden-shouldered parakeets (see below). Roomy accommodations, thus a flight at least 13 feet (4 m) long, is essential if one wants to succeed with these beautiful birds. Do not make pairs from birds born in the fall and in the spring; they will not be sexually compatible. Pair up birds that are born in the same time of the year.

Mutations: None.

Golden-shouldered Parakeet— *Psephotus chrysopterygius*

chrysopterygius: golden-winged.

Description: The top of the head is dark brown, the ear coverts are sea-green with yellow, whereas the forehead is yellowish green. The underside and flanks are light bluish-gray with green highlights. Many of the belly feathers and the lower tail feathers are red. Shoulder feathers and back are brownish-green. The back and rump are greenish-black

The Species

Psephotus chrysopterygius. The golden-shouldered parakeet is found in mainly open, lightly timbered habitats, usually where termitaria abound. Hybrids with many-colored parakeets have been bred by Sir Edward Hallstrom (Sydney); they resemble the legendary Paradise parakeet.

with white edges, as are the upper tail feathers. Secondary wing feathers are golden yellow; primaries are blue-black with lighter edges. Small wing coverts are golden yellow. The eyes are brown, the beak is blue-gray and the feet are brownish-gray. The hen is light green on the back to greenish-blue on the rump. (Note: most cocks also have a greenish-blue rump, but many wild birds have black overtones in the feathers.) The yellow in the wings is missing. All markings are vaguer and browner and the brownish-black cap is missing. The young are similar to the hen at first, but in the young males the under tail coverts and the head are darker and more intensively colored.

Size: 10¼ inches (26 cm) including the 5½-inch (14-cm) long tail. Weight: male, 2 ounces (56–58 g); female, 1⅝ ounces (54 g). Leg band: ¹³⁄₆₄ inch (5 mm).

Voice: A whistling "fweet, fweet," ending as "fwee-eep, fwee-eep." When resting, the birds utter a chattering, repeated "weet" or "feet-oo." The alarm call is a "clook, clook" (oo as in book).

Nest: In termite mounds. The hen lays three to six whitish, almost spherical eggs ⅞ by ¾ inch (22 x 19 mm) eggs. An interesting fact is that a kind of moth *(Neossiosynoeca scatophaga)* lays her eggs in the area of the nest hole; the hatching larvae feed on the droppings of the birds, keeping the floor and the feet of the nestlings clean! This is a form of symbiosis. The eggs hatch in three weeks and both parents feed the young, which leave the nest in a further five weeks.

Distribution: The subspecies *P. c. chrysopterygius* is found in the southern part of Cape York Peninsula; *P. c. dissimilis* occurs in northeastern Northern Territory (from the Arnhem Land Plateau and eastwards to the MacArthur River—Forshaw).

Remarks: This species is threatened increasingly in the wild due to its feeding grasslands being taken for agricultural purposes. Important feeding areas thus are being destroyed. During the hottest part of the day, the birds rest in the shade.

These beautiful birds do best in a large aviary with a 4-inch (10 cm) layer of sand on the floor. This should be changed regularly to keep worms and other parasites under control (see page 68). As the birds are aggressive to each other and to other species, it is best to give each pair its own accommodations. This species is recommended only for the more experienced fanciers. As they originate from a tropical climate, it is important that they are protected from cold and dampness. During the winter, they should be kept in a heated (room temperature), but roomy, enclosure.

These birds are classified as endangered by the Washington Convention and in captivity they are far from easy to breed. In the wild, they nest in the rainy season in termite mounds where, at a height of about 3.5 feet (1 m), they dig a tunnel some 19½ inches (50 cm) deep and 2 inches (5 cm) in diam-

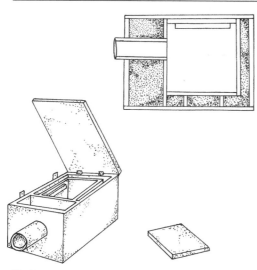

The ideal nest box for the golden-shouldered and hooded parakeets—a box within a box with insulated material in between.

eter; the inner end of the tunnel is widened out to form a nest chamber. The rain makes the termite mounds soft enough for the birds to stick their beaks into them. In the aviary we have to make a substitute for such a nest. A plywood box 9.8 by 6 by 6 inches (25 x 15 x 15 cm) can be used and a piece of 2-inch (5-cm) pvc pipe will make an entrance tunnel. The illustration shows how it is done; you will note that it is, in fact, a box *within* another box, with insulation material in between the two. Experiences of mainly European breeders have shown that when the young hatch, the hen often leaves the nest soon after; sometimes only after a couple of hours (although there are some pairs that do not leave the nest for two weeks and the young thus experience minimal danger). This behavior stems from the native habitat, where temperatures are adequate to maintain warmth in the nest. In temperate and cold climates, there is a danger that the young will be chilled and die if the hen leaves the nest too soon. Heating the nest box is therefore usually necessary—depending on the behavior of the hen. A thermostatically controlled heating element can be installed in the nest box (one that cannot be broken by the birds!). In the wild habitat, the average temperature in the breeding season is around 86° F (30° C). A good strategy is to follow the method described to me by the well-known Dutch breeder, H. Kremer:

• Three days before hatching, switch on the heater and set at 70° F (25° C).
• Two days before hatching, raise the temperature to 84° F (29° C).
• One day before hatching, raise the temperature to 91° F (33° C).
• The first two weeks after hatching, maintain at 91° F (33° C).
• The third week, set at 87.8° F (31° C).
• The fourth week, set at 84° F (29° C).
• The fifth week, set at 78.8° F (26° C).
• The following three days, set at 73.4° F (23° C).
• The following two days, reduce to 69.8° F (21° C).
• Thereafter, maintain at 64.4° F (18° C) until fledged.

After fledging, the young gradually can withstand temperatures as low as 55.4° F (13° C) but if the night temperature drops lower than 46.4° F (8° C) the young should be returned to the nest box at nightfall. Other methods of warming include the use of a heating pad or an infrared lamp near the nest box.

When the young are about four weeks old, they should be separated from the parents as the cock can get very aggressive towards them. This is contrary to wild behavior, when the young leave the nest at about five weeks and form loose groups with their parents for several weeks.

In the wild, pairs of golden-shouldered parakeets often nest close to each other. It is also helpful to aviary breeding if more than one pair are kept within hearing of each other, as a positive breeding pair can influence others to breed. The best idea is to have the breeding pairs in adjoining aviaries but with solid party walls so that the birds can hear but not see each other.

The Species

Young birds in the wild are raised on unripe seeds, so in the aviary, soaked and germinated seeds should be given as a substitute. Adult birds feed on all kinds of small grass seeds, which they forage for on the ground. Seed dishes should thus be placed on the aviary floor for captive birds. Animal proteins, derived mainly from small insects, also are necessary as well as a supply of a variety of green food—in other words, a menu similar to that described for the hooded parakeet (see page 120).

Mutations: There is a pastel mutation; a paler form of the wild color. This is very rare.

Yellow-vented Blue Bonnet— *Psephotus haematogaster*

haematogaster: blood-red belly; *haematorrhous:* with flowing blood; *pallescens:* becoming paler; *narethae:* from Naretha, a place in South Australia in the area of which the subspecies occurs.

Description: The back of the head, the breast, and the back are mainly grayish-brown; the face, edges of the wings, and the tail are blue; the belly is yellow with red and the flanks are red. The under tail coverts are deep yellow, and there is some olive-green coloring in the wings. The eyes are gray-brown, the beak is pale gray with a small, slate-gray cere; the feet are dark gray. The hen is difficult to distinguish from the cock; she has a smaller head, with less blue in the face and less red on the belly. The youngsters are similar to the adults but duller in color and with less red on the belly. They get full adult plumage after twelve months.

Size: 11 to 13⅓ inches (28–34 cm), including the 7-inch (17.5-cm) long tail. Weight: cock, 3¼ to 4 ounces (90–110 g); hen, 2½ to 3¼ ounces (75–90 g). Leg band: ¹³⁄₆₄ inch (5.4 mm).

Voice: A quickly and repeatedly uttered, two-toned chattering. Also a soft whistle as a contact call, similar to that of the pennant parakeet.

Nest: Usually in a deep tree hollow about 13 to 16 feet (4–5 m) from the ground. The hen lays four to seven, but usually five matt-white ²⁹⁄₃₂ by ¾ inch (23 x 19 mm) eggs on a layer of wood pulp and splinters. The hen incubates the eggs alone for about 21 days.

Distribution: Found in the inland of southeastern and southern Australia. There are four subspecies:

• *P. h. haematogaster:* western and southern New South Wales, northwestern Victoria, and southeastern South Australia.

• *P. h. haematorrhous,* red-vented blue bonnet: Found in southern Queensland and northern New South Wales. With deep red-colored vent feathers and reddish-brown in the wings.

• *P. h. pallescens,* pale yellow-vented blue bonnet: Found in Lake Eyre basin (South Australia). Paler colored than the type subspecies.

• *P. h. narethae,* Naretha blue bonnet: Found in southern and western Australia. Smallest race, but more intensive in color; no red on the belly, but red at the vent.

Remarks: In captivity, blue bonnets are extremely aggressive and should not be kept together with other birds, whether they are parrot-like or not as they will be sure to kill them. However a single pair kept in their own aviary with a roomy night shelter will be no trouble at all. If the pair is compatible, they will be mates for life but the cock will remain dominant over the hen. They feed on canary grass seed, various millets, grass and weed seeds, some medium striped sunflower seed, grit, a rich variety of greens and fruits and cuttlefish bone.

The first three subspecies live in pairs or small family groups on open plains, grasslands with some trees, and in arid terrain with trees and shrubs along water courses. They forage much on the ground, eating various grass seeds, insects, fruits and berries, blossoms and nectar, frequently in the shade of vegetation. If they are disturbed, they raise the crown feathers. In general these subspecies are aggressive birds and cannot be kept in a mixed collection either. Even where several pairs are in adjacent aviaries, it is advisable to have the party walls of double mesh with a space in between so that quarrels with the "neighbors" cannot become too violent! It is really best to avoid placing related species in adjacent aviaries so that breeding is not disturbed through too much excitement. The nest box is of the "grandfather clock" type with a floor area of 7.9 by 7.9 inces (20 x 20 cm) and a height of about 21⅔ inches (55 cm). The entrance hole should be 2 inches (5 cm) in diameter. Experience has shown that providing a choice of two or three nest boxes is more likely to result in success than by giving just one box. Once the hen is incubating, she will be fed by the cock; when the young are a few days old, he also will help feed them. When the young leave the nest at about five weeks of age, they are very nervous and panic easily. It is best to have plenty of twigs near each end of the flight to prevent panicky youngsters from flying into the wire mesh and injuring themselves.

In general, captive blue bonnets begin to breed early in the year; in the Netherlands, in New York (Long Island), and in Ohio, I have had blue bonnets start breeding in February. Providing that the birds are well accommodated (they can withstand quite low temperatures), early breeding should pose no problems. The incubating hen, of course, should not be disturbed. This species is scared easily from the nest, and eggs or young nestlings cannot tolerate cold conditions for long on their own. Sometimes a hen that has been shocked will abandon her clutch.

A cock blue bonnet in breeding condition can also be very aggressive to the extent that he will worry his hen excessively, sometimes with unhappy results. We can help the hen protect herself by reducing the size of the entrance hole to the nest box. This can be done by nailing a piece of tree bark over most of the hole. The hen will gnaw it so that she just fits, but the cock cannot get through. She now has a refuge for when the cock should get too attentive. Many breeders work with this method, even when cock and hen are apparently living in harmony, as it seems to give all-round better results from the hen. One easily can see when the birds are in an argumentative mood, as the males in particular raise the feathers on top of the head and nod vigorously.

I do not want to give the impression here that it is hard to make a good breeding pair with two birds of the opposite sex. Most pairs, in spite of "spells of agression," eventually will get on with each other.

Unfortunately, the yellow-vented blue bonnet is somewhat of a rarity in our aviaries; this is contrary to the subspecies red-vented blue bonnet, which is especially popular in Europe. It is a great pity that there are too many subspecific crossings, resulting in impure birds. I would thus recommend that the prospective breeder try with all his power to acquire pure specimens of any subspecies and keep the strain pure. On acquisition of birds, it is important to inspect the coloring, especially of the feathers in the area of the vent. The color must be pure and not have a pattern.

Mutations: In the wild, there seems to be a yellow mutation, but there is no further information available on this.

As mentioned above, the red-vented blue bonnet is seen more often as a guest in our aviaries. Some differences are the red on the belly, which in this subspecies runs into the the ventral tail coverts, and the wing coverts, which are reddish brown instead of olive-colored. There is little obvious difference between the sexes: the male usually has a somewhat more robust head and beak, and is perhaps a little more intensive in color. The young, on leaving the nest, already appear similar to the adults, although somewhat duller in overall color and the reddish-brown of the wings and the red of the belly is somewhat patchy for a time. As a general rule, all

Australian king parakeets usually live in pairs or small ► flocks in the forests and river margins along the east coast of Australia, where they look for seeds, berries, nectar, acorns, nuts, fruits, leaf buds, corn, and blossoms. They occasionally come to the ground to feed, but prefer to forage while clambering about in trees and large bushes. Both immature birds and adult hens have green heads.

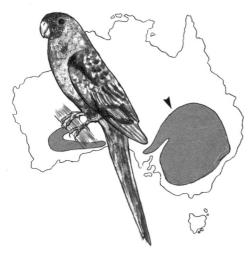

Psephotus haematorrhous. The red-vented blue-bonnet parakeet lives near water and in lightly timbered grassland and open plains in pairs or family parties. It has a harsh voice ("chack, chack") and a piping whistle, a green wing band, red upper wing coverts, and a red belly.

red-vented blue bonnets are sexually mature at twelve months of age, but do not be disappointed if it takes them a further year to produce young.

In the wild, these birds are found in areas of greater rainfall. They live in pairs or small family groups, in open woodlands and especially in trees bordering water courses. They forage mainly on the ground in search of grass seeds, herbs, insects and their larvae, nectar, flowers, berries, and fruits. When alarmed, they will raise their head feathers in a sort of mini crest.

In the aviary, give them a similar nest box as described for the yellow-vented. You also can fas-

◀ The magnificent Amboina king parakeet is from West Irian and the island of Ceram. At first the nestlings are naked, then grow a black down. The eye ring remains white. The Amboina king parakeet's mating call sounds like a flute.

ten a piece of bark over the entrance hole so that the hen can gnaw her own entry; this will the increase chances of breeding success. The hen lays four to seven eggs, which hatch in about 21 days. Although the hen will sit somewhat more tightly than the yellow-vented hen, it is still important to disturb the birds as little as possible at this time. Blue bonnets seldom raise more than one brood per season. All pairs of blue bonnets must have their own flight at least 13 to 16 feet (4–5 m) long.

A rare pastel mutation of the red-vented blue bonnet exists; this being a lighter version of the normal and probably sex-linked recessive in character.

Finally, we must discuss the subspecies Naretha or little blue bonnet, which, unlike the other blue bonnets, must be labeled as very aggressive. The sexes are difficult to distinguish. However, the hen frequently has dull blue on the head and cheek patches and more greenish blue, often not so wide as on the male, which usually has a heavier built head and beak. In contrast to the other blue bonnets, the smaller, to 11 inches (28 cm) long, Naretha has no red on the belly; this being replaced by yellow. The young are very similar to the adults, but altogether somewhat duller in color. After a number of molts, the birds gradually color up until at about four years of age there is no difference to be seen.

In the wild, Narethas live in pairs or small family groups, unlike the other blue bonnets, in dry areas but near to groups of trees. Various tree seeds (especially acacia and casuarina) form their main diet, but insects and their larvae also are taken, especially in the breeding season.

The birds breed preferably in a hollow branch or trunk of a casuarina tree; the nest opening usually being close to the ground. The nest itself can be deep down in the trunk, often below ground level in the root system.

In the aviary, a nest box 18 by 8 by 8 inches (45 x 20 x 20 cm), with an entrance hole 2 inches (5 cm) in diameter is adequate. These birds are not for the beginner; the hen is very nervous during the

Psephotus narethae. The Naretha blue-bonnet parakeet is clearly the smallest bird of the blue-bonnets. This subspecies, discovered in 1921 by F. L. Whitlock, has two-tone blue on the face, a yellow belly, and a red vent.

breeding period, and success is only likely in aviaries receiving utmost peace and quiet. Each pair should have a flight at least 13 feet (4 m) long.

Mutations: None.

Red-fronted Kakariki or Parakeet—*Cyanoramphus novaezelandia*

Cyanoramphus: blue beak; *novaezelandia:* New Zealand; *Kakariki:* the Maori name means little parakeet.

Description: The bird is mainly green in color, with lighter tones on the underside. The top and sides of the head are crimson; the hen sometimes has less red behind the eye. The adult cock does not have the violet-blue wing stripe, which the hen usually has. The primary wing feathers are blue at the tips. The beak is grayish-blue, darker at the tip; the eyes are red, the feet are gray-brown. The young are very similar to the adults, but have less red on the head, and a short tail. The beak is a little paler in color.

Size: 10¼ inches (26 cm); tail, 4⅓ to 5⅛ inches (11–13 cm). Weight: about 2⅛ ounces (60 g). Leg band: ¹³⁄₆₄ inch (5.4 mm).

Voice: These birds have a very unique and unusual voice; sometimes likened to the bleating of a goat; from which the German name for the bird "Ziegensittich" (goat parakeet) originates.

Nest: In the wild, a hollow limb or trunk of a tree is used. But on some of New Zealand's treeless islands, these birds will breed in a rock crevice or even in a hollow in the ground, often under a grass tussock. The clutch consists of three to nine (!) eggs, though most of the nests I found had three to five. The incubation period lasts 19–20 days. The hen incubates alone, but the cock regularly brings food to her and also assists later in the rearing of the young. These leave the nest in about five weeks. Kakarikis are well known as fruitful birds, which are usually sexually mature by twelve months of age. As these birds have been bred in captivity for many generations—one could say almost domesticated—hens often breed as early as four months of age after being fertilized by a three-month-old cock! However, this is not to be recommended! It is best to let young birds wait until the following season before they are allowed to breed, by not giving them any nest boxes.

Distribution: Found in New Zealand, North and South Islands, and adjacent small islands. Also occurs on Norfolk Island and New Caledonia. In New Zealand, this species is becoming rare and is now to be found only in larger wooded areas. The greatest part of their day is spent in foraging for food in the treetops or on the outer twigs of shrubs. They often also descend to the ground in search of food.

There are eight described subspecies, of which two unfortunately, are already extinct.

The Species

Cyanoramphus novaezelandia. The scarce red-fronted kakariki is a forest dweller and usually feeds on the ground, scratching the soil like a chicken! Due to the damaging behavior to large crops, the species, shot by the thousands in the nineteenth century is, fortunately, now a protected bird.

(C. n. erythrotis and *C. n. subflavescens).* It is not considered to be important to describe the differences (which are, in any case, very small) of the subspecies here, as only the nominate form is to be found in our aviaries.

Remarks: These easy-to-breed birds have become enormously popular during the last decade, not only in Europe, but also in the United States. They are very nimble in movement and clatter comfortably about the aviary wire with their long toes. They scratch on the floor like little chickens in search of tidbits. This means, unfortunately, that they are susceptible to worm infections (see page 68). This scratching also may be performed in the seed dish, so this should be constructed in such a way to make scratching impossible (use hoppers with small openings, for example).

Newly purchased birds soon will lose their nervousness, will show a friendly curiosity towards their owner, and eventually will accept tidbits from the outstretched hand. It is also good to know that these birds are far from destructive and are in no way noisy; thus they are ideal for a town aviary. A pair will soon breed, but occasionally a high death rate of the young will occur without any apparent cause. Adult birds also can die suddenly so that it is wise to obtain two unrelated pairs; then in the event of death a pair can still be made up. Not all youngsters should be sold; many fanciers form such unrelated pairs from their young for years.

Kakarikis are no problem to feed. Give them a good parakeet mixture with not too many sunflower seeds (they like them very much but too many are over fattening), plus a variety of green food. They are fond of the leaves and roots of various grasses and a daily upside down sod of grass will keep them occupied for hours. They also will eat small insects, which they find in the soil. Some individuals will eat apple, pear, grapes, peanuts, raisins, berries, mealworms, and aphids. During the breeding season, they must be given a regular supply of fresh, soaked seed, as well as a commercial rearing food suitable for grass parakeets or canaries.

Kakarikis are fond of a daily water bath; use a large, shallow dish placed on a concrete slab. The water must not be more than 2 inches (5 cm) deep, as newly fledged young (also enthusiastic bathers) otherwise could drown easily.

Breeding success is heightened by providing a not too small flight. A length of at least 13 feet (4 m) is recommended for a pair of these birds. They will indeed breed in smaller accommodations but I think these active birds deserve as much room to move about as possible. Experience has shown that a safety porch is essential on each aviary as kakarikis are quick to escape. They are clever and know when and how you enter the aviary; a secure lock is also recommended! However, escaped birds often are easy to recapture as they will stay close to the aviary—a trap cage can be used easily.

Kakarikis are best not allowed to breed in the winter as experience has shown that cold weather can cause an increased incidence of egg binding in hens. Most fanciers recommend that nest boxes should not be installed until the end of March or the beginning of April, providing of course that the weather is suitable. I also would recommend strongly that each pair should not be allowed to rear more than two broods per season.

Rosemary Low states that it is possible for a hen to rear a third brood, providing that the two earlier ones were each of not more than six individuals. More broods will reduce the hen's condition and this will be reflected in the health of the young, and these are less likely to survive in the third or fourth brood. Egg binding is also a possibility. Thus, the nest box should be removed as soon as the second brood has fledged; the hen will then usually begin to molt.

Best results occur with a nest box 13 inches (32 cm) high and 8 inches (20 cm) square. Two or three nest boxes should be given to each pair to allow a choice. Both cock and hen are involved in choosing the nest site. Once the hen accepts her future nursery, she will spend long periods inside, even sleeping in there at night.

Clutches are large and sometimes up to nine eggs. The incubation period is about 19 days, depending on the weather. At first, the hatchlings are covered in white down, but this changes to gray in a few days. The eyes open after about eight days. They leave the nest at seven to eight weeks of age and with the exception of the horn colored beak are similarly colored to their parents. Experienced fanciers already can distinguish the sexes of fledglings by the size of the beak, head, and body (Low). If the hen immediately starts a new brood, the cock will continue to feed the first youngsters. As soon as the young can feed independently, it is wise to remove them to a separate aviary as the cock can sometimes become aggressive towards them, especially his sons! Low states that of all captive psittacines, kakarikis produce the biggest clutches of eggs, and tells of a fancier in New Zealand (from where the birds originate) who had a pair that had reared 14

young in two broods and was busy rearing six more in a third brood when they were killed by rats! This same fancier possessed another pair that reared 33 young from December 1977 to December 1978. The oldest male from each of the first two broods was killed by the father, whereas another bird was killed accidentally but all the others developed into healthy specimens.

It is interesting to note that in captivity, the cock will feed the hen through the entrance hole of the nest box. As soon as the young have hatched, he will reach right inside the box to assist the hen in feeding them.

These active birds, which can run fast along their perches and climb nimbly all over the aviary mesh, have, unlike ground birds, long toes. The floor of the aviary frequently should be given a layer of leaf-mold, or, according to I. Harman, the rotted leaves of deciduous trees.

As previously stated, kakarikis are curious birds and quickly become tame. H. Kremer, the well-known Dutch breeder, told me that he had a young bird that would hang on the buttons of his jacket when he entered the aviary!

In my opinion it is sad that too many red-fronted kakarikis are paired with yellow-fronts, resulting in impure stock. These hybrids have orange on the head due to a "mixture" of yellow and red, or a combination of red and yellow feathers. Even the condition of these hybrids has declined due to too much inbreeding. It is thus important to use only strong, unrelated birds for breeding.

Finally, it is important to know that kakarikis are outstanding foster parents, as long as we don't give them young that are larger than themselves! It is also interesting that some pairs may miss out a season and not breed at all; the reason for this is unknown. The following year, successful broods will be reared by the same pair.

Mutations: There is a yellow-pied and a cinnamon mutation; both being sex-linked recessive in character. The young are born with red eyes.

The Species

Yellow-fronted Kakariki or Parakeet—*Cyanoramphus auriceps*

auriceps: golden head.

Description: This is similar in color and pattern to the preceding species, but has no red behind the eye. It has a red forehead band behind which is a yellow patch. The primary wing feathers (two to five) are blue. The eyes are reddish-brown, the beak is gray-brown, and the feet are dark gray-brown. The sexes are similar in appearance, although the cock is a little larger in build and has a brighter and wider red band and more yellow. The cock also has a redder iris, and the head and beak are more robust. Young birds are smaller and the red and yellow on the head is less obvious; the beak is horn colored. The iris is brownish. At about six months, young cocks start getting more yellow on the head. Birds should not be used for breeding until at least twelve months old.

Size: 9½ inches (24 cm); tail, 4 to 4½ inches (10–11.5 cm). Weight: about 2 ounces (55 g). Leg band: $^{13}\!/_{64}$ inch (5.4 mm).

Voice: Same as for the preceding species, but somewhat softer.

Nest: The breeding habits of this bird in the wild are poorly known, but probably are similar to the red-fronted kakariki. The hen lays five to nine eggs, which are incubated for 19 to 20 days. The cock and hen rear the young together and these leave the nest at about five weeks of age. Often (both in the wild and in captivity) a second clutch of eggs is started before the young from the preceding clutch have left the nest. In the wild, nest sites are hollow limbs or trunks of trees. A similar nest box as described for the preceding species can be used in the aviary. I strongly recommend that the birds not be allowed to have more than three broods per season as exhaustion and egg binding will result.

Distribution: Found in New Zealand and adjacent islands (North and South Island, Stewart, and Auckland). There are two subspecies documented:

C. a. auriceps and *C. a. forbesi.* The latter is somewhat larger than the type species, has paler plumage with more yellow on the belly, and the forehead band does not touch the eye. (The scientific name *forbesi* is for Dr. Henry Ogg Forbes (1851–1932), a botanist and ethnologist who led expeditions to Indonesia and New Guinea. As far as I know, this subspecies is not kept in captivity.)

Remarks: This species descends to the ground less than the red-front, and can be kept in an aviary with a length of 10 feet (3 m). They feed on a grass parakeet seed mixture and a variety of green foods, fruits, berries, insects and their larvae. In the wild, they also feed on flowers, and blossoms of various fruit trees will be taken eagerly. During the breeding season, provide a good grass parakeet/canary rearing food. Further details on management can be gleaned from the notes on the preceding species.

Australian King Parakeet—*Alisterus scapularis*

A. s. scapularis, A.s. minor.
Alisterus: Named by Gregory M. Mathews in honor of his son Alister; *scapularis:* shouldered; *minor:* smaller.

The only difference between the two subspecies is that the latter is smaller. In the aviary, it usually is difficult or impossible to tell which form one has, especially as there has been much subspecific crossing in captivity; thus destroying the unique characteristics of the subspecies.

There are three species and 11 subspecies in this genus. They are large, robust birds, with a predominance of red and green in the plumage. They are mainly dwellers of the tree foliage, but they must, of course, descend to the ground in order to drink.

King parakeets are found in the eastern part of Australia and on various islands of New Guinea to the Moluccas. In general, the hens are dominant over the cocks.

The Species

Genus	Species	Subspecies
Alisterus	*scapularis*	*scapularis*
		minor
	chloropterus	*chloropterus*
		callopterus
		moszkowski
	amboinensis	*amboinensis*
		sulaensis
		versicolor
		buruensis
		hypophonius
		dorsalis

Alisterus scapularis. The Australian king parakeet frequents the timber and thick brush-covered valleys and ranges. It communicates via its musical, soft whistle. When disturbed, the birds, which may be seen in pairs or small flocks, fly off with harsh and loud cries: "eeck, eeck, eeck."

With all subspecies of the Amboina king parakeet, there is very little sexual dimorphism; this also applies to number 5 (see Genus, Species, Subspecies listing). There are also barely any distinguishing marks in number 1–4 where the young all resemble the adult hen. In the Amboinas, however, there is a kind of juvenile plumage.

It is interesting to note that where the natural habitat of the Amboina meets that of the red-winged parakeets (numbers 1–3), there is a noticeable difference between the male and the female. Where this is not the case (numbers 4–11 inclusive), the sexes are very similar.

The same can be said about the red-winged parakeet; where these border on the habitat of the king (in Australia), cock and hen differ in color. Where the two species do not meet, then the color difference is minimal; this applies also to the Timor red-winged parakeet (*Aprosmictus j. jonquillaceus*), which occurs on the Indonesian islands of Timor and Wetar.

Description: The adult male has a red breast, throat, and head, whereas in the hen these remain green. The cock also has a light green stripe on his wings and a red upper mandible. Occasionally the hen also has the light green wing stripe.

Young birds at fledging time are very similar in color to the hen. However, the young hen's beak is usually darker in color than that of the young male. The young cock may show the beginnings of the light wing stripe and the red on his belly usually will be higher. The rump of the cock is dark blue; that of the hen is a much lighter blue.

The young male begins to change color within a year. Red feathers appear sporadically on the head and breast while the upper mandible slowly turns red. I have seen red feathers appear in October, at about six months of age. The color change occurs very slowly and cocks are often two to two and a half years old before they reach full adult coloration.

In the wild, king parakeets usually become sexually mature in their third year. Captive hens may sometimes rear young in the second year, occasionally even in their first year. However the cock must be at least two, possible three years old before he is fertile.

Size: 17 inches (43 cm). Weight: cock 7⅜ to 8 ounces (209–227 g), hen 7¾ to 9¾ ounces (220–275 g), Leg band ⁹⁄₃₂ inch (7 mm).

Voice: Their song is not unpleasant, but during flight they often let out a rather raw "eek-eek-eek-eek." When sitting alone and without being disturbed, the king parrot may whistle a soft and musical tune that can sound quite enchanting.

Nest: In the natural habitat, the nest usually is situated in a hollow limb or trunk of a large woodland tree. The nest is often quite deep within the trunk and may even be as low as ground level, although the entrance is invariably 33 feet (10 m) or more from the ground. Captive birds are very fussy in their choice of nest sites and this often has led to eggs being dropped from a perch or laid directly onto the ground.

They will prefer a deep nest box, about 6 to 6½ feet (1.8–2 m) high and with a floor area 10 by 10 inches (25 x 25 cm). The hen will prefer to be at ground level, so the nest box can be placed on the floor of the aviary. However, youngsters have been raised in suspended boxes 2 to 3 feet (60–100 cm) in height.

Three to six eggs are laid and these are brooded by the hen for about 20 days. The cock stays close and feeds her regularly. When the young are a few days old, he helps feed them. They leave the nest after about 35 days; in the wild they spend a few more weeks with the parents before grouping up with other young.

Distribution: The king parakeet occurs generally along the ranges and coastal plains of eastern Australia, to an altitude of 6,500 feet (2,000 m). It is a woodland bird that inhabits the foliage of eucalyptus and subtropical rainforest trees; however, it sometimes may be seen in more open country on agricultural land and in plantations. In spite of its mainly arboreal habit, the bird will descend to the ground to eat and to drink. Outside the breeding season, it may be seen frequently in parks and gardens in villages and towns; even in the suburbs of larger cities.

King parakeets normally live together as pairs or as small groups. In the fall, young birds may gather in groups of 20 to 30 individuals. The main part of the day is spent foraging for food or resting in the trees and shrubs. They are strong on the wing, but not so noisy and active as other Australian parakeets.

Natural food includes fruits, berries, nuts, seeds from grass and other plants, trees and shrubs, nectar, flowers, buds, insects and their larvae. They show a preference for the seeds of eucalyptus and acacia and for half-ripe maize (sweet corn). Captive birds should be given a good seed mixture, supplemented with a variety of fruits, berries, and green food.

Remarks: King parakeets are not recommended for inexperienced aviculturists. They are not too easy to breed and are fussy in the choice of partner and nesting facilities. However, they are not very aggressive and can be tamed if given the correct training. They are hardy and can withstand fairly low temperatures. They will bathe in the rain, but not in standing water. The flight should be at least 16 feet (5 m) long. If shorter, the birds will get insufficient exercise and may become lazy and inactive.

As king parakeets are woodland birds, they are not really suitable for open aviaries. A feeling of insecurity in such aviaries is perhaps a reason why the birds are not always successful in breeding. It is always best to obtain young pairs, to place them together and to make no further changes to the aviary, except to give them a choice of nest boxes when the time is ripe.

Mutations: A yellow mutation (not a lutino) is known, but this is very rare. It is a beautiful bird in which the red plumage stays red but all of the green feathers become yellow. In young cocks, the head and belly are first yellow. It is an autosomal recessive mutation.

There have been cases of adult cock birds changing their red color to orange. The reason for this is unknown. The offspring are normal in color.

The Species

Green-winged King Parakeet—
Alisterus chloropterus

A. c. chloropterus, A. c. callopterus, A. c. moszkowskii.

Moszkowskii: after Max Moszkowski, a German doctor, born in 1873 who collected animals and plants in New Guinea, among other places, including this bird, *chloropterus*: green-winged; *callopterus*: beautiful-wings.

Description: It is easy to distinguish the sexes of the Moszkowski king parakeet as the hen lacks the blue back of the cock. The young are similar to the hen, but the light green wing stripe is narrower and duller in color and the breast is greener. They became sexually mature in their third year. At two

Alisterus chloropterus. The green-winged king parakeet inhabits eastern New Guinea, and is sexually dimorphic. The bird was first shown at the London Zoo in 1909.

years of age, the sexes of the young are still difficult to distinguish.

The hen of *moszkowskii* has almost no blue on the back. The cock of the subspecies *A.c. callopterus* is similar to that of the *A.c. moszkowskii*. In *A.c. chloropterus*, the blue of the back runs up into the neck and the wing stripe is more yellowish-green. The hens of the *A.c. chloropterus* and *A.c. callopterus* are similar to the Australian king parakeet, having a green head and breast, but they differ in having a little red on the upper mandible.

Size: 14 inches (36 cm). Leg band: ⁹⁄₃₂ inch (7 mm).

Nest: Little is known of the breeding habits of this species. In the aviary, it will use a nest-box similar to other king parakeets (height of about 6 feet (180 cm) and a floor area of 10 by 10 inches (25 x 25 cm) with a 3.5 inch (9 cm) entrance hole).

Two or three eggs are laid, and these take about 20 days to hatch. The young of captive-bred specimens have stayed in the nest for 42, 49, and 56 days. The hen may lay again immediately, but the eggs are not always fertile.

Distribution: This species was first discovered in 1878 by Dr. Ramsay in the eastern mountain district of Australian New Guinea (now Papua New Guinea). These birds are of the lowland and foothill forests of the islands that they inhabit. They seem to prefer lower trees or lower branches of large trees, rarely ascending to the canopy. They are naturally peaceful birds and will allow one to approach quite closely. They usually are seen singly or in groups of two or three individuals.

Seeds, berries, nuts, fruits, leaves, flowers, and similar foods are all on the menu. They require more fruit and green food than their Australian relatives—especially in the case of newly imported birds.

Remarks: Great care must be taken with newly imported birds; especially as they are not frequently available to the aviculturist. They come from a warm, humid habitat and are accustomed to copious amounts of soft food. The change from fruit and

The Species

berries to hard seeds can cause intestinal problems, so plenty of soft food must be offered. Care in acclimatization is also important; birds must not be placed in unheated outdoor aviaries during the colder parts of the year.

Once accustomed to a new diet and acclimatized, these birds are quite as hardy as the Australian king parakeet and can overwinter in unheated outdoor aviaries (with a draft- and damp-proof shelter).

Mutations: None.

Amboina King Parakeet—*Alisterus amboinensis*

A. a. amboinensis: Amboinia king parakeet; *A. a. sulaensis*: Sula king parakeet; *A. a. versicolor*: Peleng king parakeet; *A. a. buruensis*: Buru king parakeet; *A. a. hypophonius*: Halmahera king parakeet; *A. a. dorsalis*: Sulawati king parakeet.

There is a marked difference between the Amboina and the Hamahera king parakeet: the former has green wings, the latter has blue. The other subspecies are never or almost never available to aviculturists and are thus not further described here. *Amboinensis*: from the island of Ambon; *sulaensis*: from the island of Sula; *versicolor*: various colors; *hypophonius*: blood-red beneath; *dorsalis*: of the back.

Ambon, Sula, Peleng, Buru, Halmahera, and Sulawati are all Indonesian islands.

Description: Males and females are difficult to tell from each other, but there may be some difference in the sizes of the heads and beaks. The young are also similar to the adults, but have no blue on the back. The upper mandible is brownish-black, the lower mandible is reddish, and the eye ring is whitish rather than gray. This changes in the first year. They are sexually mature in the third year.

Size: Amboina, 16 inches (41 cm); Buru, 15½ inches (50 cm); Halmahera, 14½ inches (37 cm); Sulawati, 15 inches (38 cm). Leg band: 9⁄32 inch (7 mm).

Alisterus amboinensis. The Amboina king parakeet lives in the wild, primarily eating fruits, berries, buds, and seeds. Several races are recognized; they all live on various Indonesian islands.

Nest: The Amboina king parakeet has been bred in nest boxes from four to six feet (120–180 cm) high and a floor area 10 to 12 inches (25–30 cm) square. The entrance hole should be about 3½ inches (9 cm) across.

Two or three eggs are laid and these are brooded by the hen alone for about 19 days. In Denmark, a hen laid eggs on the first and third of July; both hatched on July 21 and the young left the nest on September 7, thus after 48 days. Other examples reported include times ranging from 56–63 days. Sometimes two broods are reared and not always in the spring. When the young reach fourteen days of age, the cock will help the hen feed them; before that he only feeds the hen. The hen is noticeably more aggressive when she has young and may sometimes attack the cock. In such cases, it is best to remove the cock from the aviary and let the hen rear the young on her own.

Distribution: These birds are found only on a number of Indonesian islands. They are by no means numerous in the wild and are therefore quite scarce in aviculture.

Like the green-winged king parakeet, they inhabit the forests of the lowlands and foothills of the ranges. Singly or in pairs, they forage in the thicker lower vegetation of the trees, but rarely descend to the ground.

Their diet is similar to that of the green-winged king parakeet: seeds, berries, fruit, leaves, flowers, and possibly insects and their larvae. In the aviary, they must be given a rich variety of fruit, berries, seeds, and green food, including chickweed, spinach, and ears of sweet corn.

Remarks: As with the green-winged parakeet, care must be taken in acclimatization and food changeover. Acclimatized birds are fairly hardy and can withstand some frost.

It may take newly imported birds up to five years to come into breeding condition. These parakeets like to fly a lot, but they hardly gnaw.

Mutations: None.

Cockatiel—*Nymphicus hollandicus*

nymphicus: like a nymph; *hollandicus*: Gmelin used the scientific name appropriately, because Australia was known as New Holland at that time (1788).

Description: The male is grayish blue. The head and crest are yellow. Ear markings are orange-yellow. There are white wing coverts. The yellow on the head and crest is less bright in the female. The ear markings are darker; the white wing coverts are somewhat grayish. The eyes are brown, the beak is grayish-blue, and the feet are dark gray.

Size: 12 to 13 inches (30–33 cm); tail 5½ to 6⅔ inches (14–17 cm). Weight: cock, 2⅝ to 3⅔ ounces

Nymphicus hollandicus. The cockatiel is nomadic and was once extremely numerous.

(80–102 g); hen, 3⅛ to 3¼ ounces (89–92 g). Leg band: about ¹³⁄₆₄ inch (5.4 mm)

Voice: Cockatiels whistle the entire day, and the male in particular is capable of perfectly imitating all kinds of other bird songs. A colleague once wrote me. "All the while I was thinking that my Pekin Robin was whistling his tune when I noticed that it was my cockatiel which was singing so beautifully. When I go to feed my cockatiel, he will bravely remain on his perch, even when I am just a foot away from him. Finally, I am so close that his bill is near my forehead. If, at this close range, I then whistle to him—like exchanging so much gossip—he always answers me by whistling the same tune back to me."

Nest: In hollow limbs or holes in thick branches or tree trunks of (mainly) eucalyptus; sometimes only 3 feet (1 m) above the ground. Sometimes

The Species

more than one nest is found per tree. In the wild as well as in captivity, cockatiels are excellent breeders. The hen lays four to seven, normally four to five, 1.1 by ⅞ inch (28 x 22 mm) eggs, which take 20 days to hatch. The male sits on them during the day, and the female at night. When the young are approximately 30 days old, they leave the nest but will continue to be fed by both parents for some time. The floor of the nesting box should measure 10 by 10 inches (25.5 x 25.5 cm); the height; 1 foot (30 cm), the entrance should have a diameter of 3.5 inches (9 cm), placed about 2.5 inches (6.5 cm) beneath the roof. Cockatiels are not fussy about the form of their nursery, and you can use old (but not warped) wood less than 1 inch (1.9 cm) thick to construct nest boxes that should last for many years. Just below the entrance hole, fix a perch 7 inches (18 cm) long and about ⅝ inch (1.5 cm) in diameter, so that it protrudes both inside and outside the nest box. The box floor can be covered with a 1.5 to 2 inch (4–5 cm) layer of damp peat, mixed with a few wood shavings. In the middle of this layer, press a hollow with your fist to create a place where the hen can later place her eggs. This depression prevents the eggs from rolling about too much.

Distribution: Found in Australia, particularly in the interior, but rarer along the coastal regions. Imported into Tasmania, though their wanderings apparently also have led them there.

Remarks: Their menu should consist of the following: panicum millet, canary grass seed, oats, lots of greens (particularly when there are young in the nest), especially privet leaves, eggs, soaked seeds, bread, a few mealworms, ant eggs, and slices of apples and carrots. The young, which resemble the female initially, often stick their little heads out of the nest, making a peeping "sissing" noise. It is

a good idea to make the nesting box so the bird sitting on the eggs will have its head at the height of the box opening; do not make the opening too high up. Place a thick layer of peat and wood shavings on the bottom of the box. In any case, do not use a nesting box where the entrance is too low, because cockatiels have the habit of leaving the nest when they are startled. When the bird on the nest has the opportunity to see everything that is happening around him or her, you will experience little trouble with deserted nests. You can be sure of good breeding results only when you house your birds in a roomy aviary by themselves. It speaks for itself that you should not disturb them when they are breeding; nest inspections, therefore, should be avoided unless you happen to have hand tamed birds that are not bothered by your peeking in the "nursery." If your garden aviary has a good night shelter, you can leave your cockatiels outside during the winter. Finally, I would like to point out that cockatiels often make outstanding foster parents for *Platycercus* and other Australian parakeet species.

Mutations: During the last few years, the breeding of color mutations in cockatiels has attracted a great deal of attention. Well-known mutations are pied (harlequin or variegated), which is autosomal recessive, as is silver, white face (charcoal), and fallow. The pearl (laced or opaline) is sex-linked recessive, but after 6 to 12 months the males molt into normal (= wild color) gray adult plumage. The females retain their pearl markings. The cinnamon (fawn or isabel) is also sex-linked recessive. Cinnamons, like the autosomal recessive fallows, are born with red eyes. However, the cinnamons get dark eyes within a week, whereas the fallows retain their red eyes. The lutino and albino are both sex-linked recessive.

Useful Addresses and Literature

United States

American Federation of Aviculture (AFA)
P.O. Box 1568
Redondo Beach, California 90278
Association of Avian Veterinarians
P.O. Box 299
East Northport, New York 11731
Avicultural Society of America, Inc.
8228 Sulphur Road
Ojai, California 93023
National Parrot Association
8 North Hoffman Lane
Hauppauge, New York 11788
The Society of Parrot Breeders and Exhibitors
P.O. Box 369-CB
Groton, Massachusetts 01450

Great Britian

The Avicultural Society
Warren Hill, Halford's Lane
Hartley Wintney, Hampshire RG27 8AG
The European Aviculture Council
P.O. Box 74
Bury St. Edmunds, Suffolk IP30 OHS
National Council for Aviculture
87 Winn Road
Lee, London SE12 9EY

Canada

The Canadian Avicultural Society
32 Dronmore Court
Willodale, Ontario M2R 2H5
Canadian Parrot Association
Pine Oaks R.R. #3
St. Catharines, Ontario L2R 6P9

Australia

The Avicultural Society of Australia
52 Harris Road
Elliminyt, Victoria 3249

New Zealand

Avicultural Society of N.Z., Inc.
P.O. Box 21
403 Henderson, Auckland

Books

Forshaw, J. *Australian Parrots*, 2nd edition. Landsdowne Editions, 1981.
——, *Parrots of the World*, 3rd edition. Landsdowne Editions, 1989.
Groen, Dr. H. D. *Australian Parakeets*, 5th edition. Audubon Publishing Co., New York, 1987.
Hutchins, B. R. and R. H. Lovell. *Australian Parrots, A Field and Aviary Study*, revised edition. Avicultural Society of Australia.
Kolar, Kurt. *Parrots*. Barron's Educational Series, Inc., Hauppauge, New York, 1990.
Vriends, Dr. M. M. *The New Bird Handbook*. Barron's Educational Series, Inc., Hauppauge, New York, 1989.
——, *The New Cockatiel Handbook*. Barron's Educational Series, Inc., Hauppauge, New York, 1989.

Magazines

American Cage Bird Magazine
One Glamore Court
Smithtown, New York 11787

The A.F.A. Watchbird
P.O. Box 56218
Phoenix, Arizona 85079-6218

Bird Talk
P.O. Box 6050
Mission Viejo, California 92690

Bird World
P.O. Box 70
N. Hollywood, California 91603

Cage and Aviary Birds
Prospect House
9-13 Ewell Road
Cheam, Surrery SM1 499
England

CITES

Treaty Regulates Trade

The United States and 98 other countries are signatories of the Convention on International Trade in Endangered Species, or CITES Treaty, which was designed to regulate the import, export, or re-export in those species of wildlife (plants and animals) considered to be endangered or subject to heavy demands.

There are three lists (Appendixes) that indicate the level of protection assigned to a particular species. Each party nation to this convention must have a Management Authority (MA) and a Scientific Authority (SA). In the United States, we have a combined office, operating in the U.S. Fish and Wildlife Service, Department of the Interior.

The three listings are:

Appendix I:

Lists all endangered plant and animal species (for example, the orange-bellied grass parakeet!), and none may be traded in international commerce for commercial purposes.

Obtain a Permit

You may purchase birds that are listed as endangered, if you obtain a permit to do so.

Normally permits will be issued for the purchase of birds that legally have entered the United States or were captive-bred here, if the purchaser intends to breed the birds or has some equally serious purpose.

Write to:

Federal Wildlife Permit Office
1000 Glebe Road
Arlington, Virginia 22201

You may also write for leaflets that explain the laws dealing with the sale or purchase of endangered species. If you have specific questions, you may telephone (703) 235-1905.

Shipments require two primarily noncommercial permits: one from the importing country (and obtained first), and the other from the country of export. The import must not be detrimental to the survival of the species.

Appendix II:

Lists species not presently endangered, but which may become so unless trade is strictly regulated. Import permits are not needed, but export permits are required for Appendix II species when the SA of the exporting country finds that trade in the particular species is nondetrimental to the survival of the species in the wild. Permits must indicate, by number, the common and scientific names of each species in the shipment. If the shipment contains specimens that are being re-exported and/or captive-bred, documents must reflect such status.

Captive-bred or artificially propagated Appendix I specimens produced for commercial purposes are treated as if they are Appendix II species. Significant trade in Appendix II species is monitored by CITES to determine if those species should be up-listed to Appendix I or if other measures are required.

Appendix III:

Lists plant and animal species regulated for wildlife conservation reasons by a CITES party to assist in listing the party's domestic controls. International shipment requires either an export permit from the country that lists the species on Appendix III or a re-export certificate or certificate of origin from any other country. No import permits are required. The MA must determine the legality and enforce proper shipment methods.

If you would like complete copies of the above regulations, write to:

Office of Management Authority
United States Fish and Wildlife Service
P.O. Box 27329
Washington, D.C. 20038-7329

Ask for 50 CFR 23, 50 CFR 17, and 50 CFR 13. Also ask for the most recent CITES list and a current Endangered and Threatened Wildlife and Plants Publication. All are free.

Index

Boldface numbers indicate color photos.

Index